MW00641278

GUNS FOR COTTON
ENGLAND ARMS THE CONFEDERACY

Thomas Boaz

BURD STREET PRESS

Copyright © 1996 by Thomas M. Boaz

ALL RIGHTS RESERVED — No part of this book may be reproduced in any
form without permission in writing from the publisher, except by a reviewer
who wishes to quote brief passages in connection with a review.

This Burd Street Press publication
was printed by
Beidel Printing House, Inc.
63 West Burd Street
Shippensburg, PA 17257 USA

In respect for the scholarship contained herein, the acid-free paper used in this
book meets the guidelines for permanence and durability of the Committee on
Production Guidelines for Book Longevity of the Council on Library Resources.

For a complete list of available publications
please write
White Mane Publishing Company, Inc.
P.O. Box 152
Shippensburg, PA 17257 USA

Library of Congress Cataloging-in-Publication Data

Boaz, Thomas, 1943-
        Guns for cotton : England arms the Confederacy / Thomas Boaz.
        p.   cm.
        Includes bibliographical references and index.
        ISBN 1-57249-004-7
        1. Confederate States of America--Relations--Great Britain.
2. Great Britain--Relations--Confederate States of America.
3. Confederate States of America--Commerce--Great Britain. 4. Great
Britain--Commerce--Confederate States of America. 5. Military
assistance, British--Confederate States of America. 6. United
States--History--Civil War, 1861-1865--Economic aspects. I. Title.
E488.B63   1996
973.7'1--dc20   95-53817
                                                                                                      CIP

PRINTED IN THE UNITED STATES OF AMERICA

*This book is dedicated to
my wife, Barbara,
who was a cheerful advisor and helper,
and to our daughter, Tory.*

TABLE OF CONTENTS

List of Illustrations vi

Introduction viii

Chapter 1. The Confederate States in 1861 1

Chapter 2. Blockade and Response 6

Chapter 3. Organizing International Supply Operations 11

Chapter 4. The Pipeline Fills 15

Chapter 5. The View From England 19

Illustrations 23

Chapter 6. Arms and Controversy. 46

Chapter 7. Government Finance and Control 53

Chapter 8. Blockade Running From the Islands 58

Chapter 9. Best-Clad Army in the World 64

Conclusion. 68

Epilogue 70

Appendix. 74

Endnotes 76

Further Resources 80

Bibliography 81

Index. 85

LIST OF ILLUSTRATIONS

George Alfred Trenholm 23

Col. Josiah Gorgas, Chief of Ordnance, C.S.A. 24

Capt. Caleb Huse, C.S.A. in later life 25

A British army M1853 "Enfield" 0.577 calibre rifle-musket
with its bayonet. 25

The *Bermuda's* extensive manifest from a voyage in early 1862. 26

Commander James Dunwoody Bulloch, C.S.N. 28

An Erlanger Certificate 29

One of the Laird Rams 30

The blockade runner *Hope.* 30

Stephen R. Mallory, Secretary of the Confederate States Navy. 31

The *Col. Lamb*, sister ship to the *Hope* 32

The cotton compresses on the docks at Wilmington 32

Blockade runners *Nashville* and *Tuscarora* 33

A Confederate blockade runner enters the harbor at Nassau. 34

"No. 294," also known as *El Tousson* 35

Fort Fisher shortly after its fall to United States forces. 36

Fort Fisher, commanding the new inlet entrance to Cape Fear River. 36

Confederate ironclad rams engage United States blockade ships 37

England's "friendly neutrality" toward the South 38

A sarcastic view of the North ("Brother Jonathan") 39

List of illustrations

Map showing the interior 40

Charleston, South Carolina, and its harbor in early 1861. 41

The steamship shown on this Confederate $1 dollar bill 42

Jefferson Davis' optimistic speeches 42

James Mason and John Slidell, Confederate commissioners..................... 43

The *Oreto* sailed to the Bahamas where she received her armament. 43

A British musket cap pouch 44

British army wooden canteen 44

A British military knapsack 44

Men of the 44th Massachusetts Infantry 45

INTRODUCTION

The Confederate government imported vast amounts of military supplies from Europe, but it was the supply line from England that was vital to sustaining the Confederate army and navy. Moreover, just a handful of dedicated men were responsible for the flow of arms and equipment of all types that entered the South.

According to an article in the August 1864 issue of the New York *Historical Magazine,* Confederate soldiers were nicknamed "Johnnies" because they received so many supplies from England, the land of the mythical John Bull. Today, however, the importance of Anglo-Confederate operations, and of the men who ran them, is obscured in comparison to the battles and personalities of the War Between the States. This book is therefore intended to be a general introduction to that complex topic, with a focus upon operations in the Southeast.

It should be noted that the Confederate government's foreign and domestic finances were quite intricate, that Gulf coast ports were also active blockade running centers, and that continental Europe was an essential source of military equipment. Those areas are beyond the scope of this book, but the Further Resources section and the bibliography provide extensive references for those wishing additional information about Confederate foreign supply.

A number of individuals and organizations assisted with the preparation of this book. In particular, I wish to thank Philip Katcher for his invaluable help with a number of important matters. Also, Ethel Nepveux shared information about her distinguished ancestor, George Alfred Trenholm; Barbara L. Rowe and Timothy S. Bottoms of the Cape Fear Museum in Wilmington, North Carolina, assisted with some of the illustrations, as did Steven J. Wright at the Civil War Library and

Museum in Philadelphia and Gehrig Spencer of Fort Fisher Historic Site; Larry Walsh of the Limerick Museum in Ireland was a source of details about Peter Tait and his company; Charles W. Smithson in Princeton provided a copy of an Erlanger certificate. I also acknowledge the contributions of the Museum of the Confederacy, Richmond; Bermuda Archives; City of London Libraries and Art Galleries; National Army Museum, London; Lloyd's of London; and the Confederate Historical Society of Great Britain.

CHAPTER ONE

The Confederate States in 1861

WHEN the Civil War began, the South's population was about nine million, roughly a third of whom were slaves. Although industrialization had begun in the region, the Confederate States of America were for the most part rural and agrarian. Within the borders of the thirteen states were just two of the nine cities of the former United States with populations over 100,000,[1] and just 14 percent of its industry.

At the same time, the North was developing into an industrial colossus, powered by the hordes of arriving immigrants who provided cheap labor for the mills and factories. Those people brought with them their own customs and religions, and the character of the North began to change. Southerners who visited there often felt they were in a strange country.

Southern society was different. White Southerners were overwhelmingly Anglo-Saxon and Protestant, and to a great extent the South of 1861 retained much of the distinctions and traditions of the agrarian society brought over from Britain in the eighteenth century. Southern attitudes were also different from those in the North, and often filled with paradoxes. They were a devoutly Christian people, yet those who were able to indulge themselves saw no conflict in pursuing an extraordinarily hedonistic lifestyle. Breeding, dash, and good manners were valued far more than excessive commercial zeal, and thus their region suffered from a lack of capital improvements. An overwhelmingly agrarian people, they had both a reverential attachment to the land and the carelessness to wear it out with unenlightened farming methods.

Thus, on the brink of war the South was a region unto itself, whose people took pride in their own traditions and laissez-faire agricultural economy. Louis T. Wigfall, a Confederate senator, hardly exaggerated

1

the situation to a correspondent from the London *Times*: "We are a pe-
culiar people, sir!" We have no cities—we don't want them. We have no
literature—we don't need any yet... We want no manufactures: we de-
sire no trading, no mechanical or manufacturing classes. As long as we
have our rice, our sugar, our tobacco, and our cotton, we can command
wealth to purchase all we want."[2]

As Wigfall noted, in contrast with the new industrial fortunes being made in the North, Southern wealth continued to be based upon the
ownership of land and the production of the key money crops of cotton,
tobacco and turpentine. Of those, cotton was by far the most valuable
crop, and production of the fiber exploded when newly established plan-
tations in Arkansas, Louisiana, Mississippi and Texas increased cotton
output from less than two million bales in 1848 to more than 4.5 million
bales by 1860.

By that time, Southern production accounted for almost 90 percent of the world's supply of cotton. However, because of a lack of significant milling capability within its own region, Southern cotton was
sold to mills in the North and exported in great quantity to the booming
cotton milling industry in England.

Just prior to the outbreak of hostilities, the annual value of Southern cotton exports to England alone had grown to about $150 million.[3]
There, twelve hundred factories and mills consumed more than four
times the amount of cotton used in Northern mills. The English milling
industry produced vast amounts of finished cotton goods that were sold
around the world, and directly or indirectly the industry provided the
livelihoods of some five million English men, women and children, one-
sixth of the country's population. Even the French milling industry,
though smaller and more specialized than in England, looked to the
South for 93 percent of its supply of raw cotton.

Cotton accounted for some 60 percent of the total value of all United
States exports,[4] and Southerners proudly boasted that "Cotton is King."
Charleston, Mobile, and other Southern ports prospered with international trade as businesses around the world became increasingly de-
pendent upon an uninterrupted flow of cotton. Strong commercial links
were established between financial and shipping firms on both sides of
the Atlantic, and those relationships would later become an invaluable
asset to the Confederacy.

South Carolina seceded from the Union on December 20, 1860. By
the following May there were eleven states in the Confederacy, and by
the end of the year Kentucky and Missouri had been admitted. However, despite the political upheavals and the possibility of war, Southern planters and merchants delivered the 1860 cotton crop to buyers in
the North and Europe under preexisting contracts.[5] By the end of May

1861, some 3.6 million bales of cotton—almost the entire current crop— had been exported.

Nevertheless, the prevailing Southern view was that while the North might be an industrial colossus better prepared to fight a war, the Confederacy retained the prime advantage—cotton. The belief in King Cotton led many in the South to conclude that the crop was so vitally important to maintaining their economies that England and France would let nothing, including war with the North, interfere with the flow of cotton to their mills. It was assumed that simply withholding cotton would quickly force political recognition of the new Confederacy from the two countries.

To intensify the question of foreign assistance, in 1861 Southern planters initiated a voluntary but widespread embargo against cotton shipments to England and France. Because the South had no significant merchant marine, it was hoped this action would force the two nations to send their own ships through the Northern blockade in order to obtain cotton at Southern ports. Any interference with their ships by the United States Navy might force Britain and France into direct intervention on behalf of the South.

Initially, many Southerners thought that the industrial might of the North could be nullified by a gallant Confederacy backed by the two most powerful nations on earth. However, coercing European aid by withholding the lifeblood of their cotton mills was a doomed idea from the beginning. The 1859 and 1860 cotton crops had been quite large, and by early 1861 English mills were overstocked with both raw cotton and unsold finished products. As well, some two hundred thousand bales of unsold cotton still remained in Southern warehouses. At the time, those bales could have been easily shipped through the blockade to England for storage; instead, they were withheld until the Union blockade became dangerously strong.

Thus, it was almost two crucial years before English mills were severely pressed for new supplies of raw cotton. The larger mills themselves were able to stay in operation on reduced schedules, but the embargo caused great hardships among the workers. Layoffs began almost immediately, and unemployment among English mill workers quickly rose. At the peak of the "Cotton Famine" in 1863, almost 40 percent of workers in some districts were unemployed and on relief.[6] The easing of the workers' crisis did not occur until the South was ultimately forced to ship its cotton abroad in payment for supplies.

From a practical aspect, the Confederate States of America started without any real depth as a nation. The early cotton-based diplomacy created tensions between the British and Confederate governments, while at the same time, domestic matters were also in disarray.

Jefferson Davis was inaugurated as president of the Confederate States of America on February 18, 1861. The new government, then headquartered in Montgomery, Alabama, literally began with nothing. The spacious Montgomery Insurance Building, even devoid of furniture, became "Government House," where departmental names were simply written on cardboard and pinned to doorposts. Officials acquired rudimentary furnishings and such basic supplies as stationery from local merchants.[7]

The government's finances consisted only of the $718,294.08 seized from Federal custom houses and mints in Charlotte and New Orleans, and a pledge of some $500,000 from the state of Alabama. Militarily, conditions were not much better. In April, Major Josiah Gorgas, head of the Confederate Ordnance Bureau, reported that the available stocks of military hardware were marginal. On hand were only about 164,000 small arms of assorted types and calibers, many of which were antique flintlocks, 3.2 million cartridges, and some nine hundred cannon of various types and ages.[8]

That same month, Quartermaster General Abraham C. Myers ordered five thousand sets of uniforms from New Orleans contractors. When he increased the order and asked mills in Georgia and Virginia to help uniform the influx of volunteers, it became obvious that domestic raw materials and factories were inadequate to supply a large army. His recommendation to import uniforms and equipment from Europe was ignored by Secretary of War Leroy Pope Walker.

The government moved quickly to obtain funds for its initial operations by the sale of Confederate government "loans." In February 1861, at the peak of fervent patriotism, the government announced the issuance of a $15 million loan with a twenty-year maturity. It paid 8 percent interest and was backed by duties on cotton that was allowed to be exported.

On March 16, Secretary of the Treasury Christopher G. Memminger announced that the first $5 million portion of the loan would be sold on April 17. That news was enthusiastically received by the public, and the loan was heavily oversubscribed within nine days. The balance was placed with equal ease during the next several months. While the loan provided the government with short-term operating capital, it also had the unintended consequence of draining a great deal of the individually held currency out of the banks to pay for the bonds.

The success of that issue led to a $50 million loan several months later, marketed principally to farmers and planters who could exchange their cotton, tobacco, and other crops for the bonds since specie was scarce. The popular "Produce Loan" was followed by a series of similar loans that totaled some $300 million by the end of 1863.[9] Part of the proceeds of those loans and bond issues funded the purchase program in England for several years, but the rampant inflation caused by the issuance of so much currency, notes and bonds, ultimately forced a change in how foreign purchases were financed.

By 1863, Confederate bonds and notes were sinking in value. English merchants, many of whom were sympathetic to the South, began to demand hard cash or other suitable methods of payment for military supplies. Satisfying those demands used up much of the limited stock of specie on hand, and often resulted in long delays in obtaining supplies or in getting them shipped into the South. The lack of hard cash soon became at least as great a problem for the Confederate agents in England as was the blockade itself—until English guns were exchanged for Southern cotton.

At the onset, the Confederacy was able only to sustain a quick war where courage, determination, and gallantry would carry the day. As Mary Chestnut wrote in her diary: "If it could all be done in one wild desperate dash, we could do it. But...we can [not] stand the long bleak months between acts—waiting."[10]

The meager industrial capacity of the South meant that military supplies of all types had to obtained overseas. The Confederate government was faced with having to rely upon foreign sources for military equipment at a time when government finances were unsteady and there was neither a merchant marine to transport the goods nor a navy to protect Southern ships and ports. Given such daunting obstacles, the subsequent development of the transatlantic military supply line was remarkable in scope.

CHAPTER TWO

Blockade and Response

AT the same time Myers was urging the importation of Confederate uniforms, President Abraham Lincoln was contemplating a blockade of Southern ports. However, two of his key advisors, Attorney General Edward Bates and Secretary of War Gideon Welles, recommended that the ports be closed rather than blockaded, because in their view a blockade was an act of war which a nation could not commit upon itself. By blockading Southern ports, they argued, the Federal government would not only automatically give the Confederacy the status of a belligerent nation, but there could be damaging problems with foreign governments if their ships and cargoes were seized by blockading United States warships.

Lincoln prevailed, and declared a blockade in effect as of April 19, 1861. His plan was fraught with danger, however, as other nations were not obliged to recognize a blockade until the ports in question were actually sealed off by ships on station. Under international law, the mere proclamation of a blockade was not sufficient to prevent foreign ships from attempting to enter Southern ports. Moreover, when the blockade was declared, the United States Navy consisted only of some ninety ships, of which forty-two were out of commission with the remainder being either in foreign ports or at sea.[1] It was a woefully inadequate force to blockade more than 3,500 miles of southern coastline and its nearly two hundred rivers, bays, harbors, and inlets.

As well, since the entire cotton crop had previously been shipped and the next one wouldn't be ready until the fall of 1862, Lincoln incurred a substantial risk that if a severe cotton shortage developed in England it might cause the Royal Navy to open the blockaded ports by force. "The blockade question we consider to be the great lever which will eventually decide the relations between Europe and the South," wrote Confederate foreign commissioners William L. Yancey and A. Dudley Mann in July 1861.[2]

The United States Navy immediately began an aggressive course to construct, lease, or purchase as many ships as possible. The fleet doubled in size within a year and grew to over six hundred ships by war's end, but for the first year the blockade was quite porous. Had Southern cotton planters not decided to embargo cotton shipments, that first year provided a perfect opportunity for them to have easily shipped their cotton to England.

The declaration of blockade allowed England to declare itself neutral, and to grant both North and South the rights of belligerents. That was of great importance to the Richmond government, as it could now buy arms, equipment, and ships overseas. Likewise, as neutral nations, England and France could buy Southern cotton, which would not have been possible if the ports were merely closed.

On April 30, 1861, Norfolk was the first port to be blockaded. By the end of July Charleston, Galveston, New Orleans, Mobile, Savannah, and Wilmington were also under blockade, albeit rather ineffectively. A Charleston woman noted in her diary for July that "They [blockading ships] do not so effectively shut us out as they suppose, for Privateermen slip past them every dark night both to & from the West Indies." [3]

Having no navy of its own, the Confederate response in May was to issue Letters of Marque and Reprisal to privateers. After posting bonds of between $5,000 to $10,000, depending upon the size of their ships and crews, owners of private vessels were authorized to capture Northern merchant ships and sell the cargoes, the profits of which they could retain. They were also to receive 20 percent of the value of any captured United States Navy ships.

President Davis was convinced the scheme would work, saying that "A small fleet [of privateers] hovering on the coast of the Northern states, capturing and destroying their vessels, [would fill] the enemy with consternation."[4] However, being confined mainly to the shores and rivers of the South, and with few qualified ships, the "militia of the seas" took only some fifty small prizes. Except as a temporary morale booster, privateers never had a significant impact.

A far more effective response had been recommended by the brilliant Stephen R. Mallory, Secretary of the Confederate Navy. A Floridian, Mallory had been a United States senator, serving in the important role of chairman of the Senate's Committee on Naval Affairs. He resigned from the Senate in January 1861, becoming Secretary of the Confederate Navy two months later. An Anglophile and bon vivant, he was also widely regarded as a far-seeing expert in naval developments, and well understood the limited ability of the South to build its own navy.

Mallory quickly responded to the blockade with an innovative plan: he would obtain a small but extremely powerful and technologically advanced Confederate navy from foreign sources. Of greatest importance to him were ironclad ships. Both England and France had been experimenting with that revolutionary design in warships, and Mallory felt that a fleet of forty such ships could break the blockade, badly damage the United States Navy, and create havoc in the civilian population by raiding Northern port cities.

He requested them on April 26, saying that the government should "adopt a class of vessels hitherto unknown...a combination of the greatest known floating battery and power of resistance...Vessels of this character and capacity cannot be found in this country and must be purchased abroad."

Mallory also wanted six armed steam cruisers, equally capable of destroying United States commercial shipping on the high seas and engaging blockade ships along the Southern coast. His plan was ambitious, but he believed that the navy the South was unable to build could be acquired in England, if all went well.

On May 9 Mallory ordered thirty-eight-year-old Commander James Dunwoody Bulloch to England with several missions. First, at his discretion, he was to either construct or purchase the six steam cruisers. Second, to begin arrangements for the construction of the ironclad ships. Lastly, to fulfill general orders to obtain various weapons and equipment useful to the Confederate navy and marines. The list included such items as "10,000 good Enfield rifles, or rifled muskets, with bayonets for the navy."[5]

About a week later, Mallory sent Lieutenant James H. North of the Confederate navy to France in an attempt to purchase the armored frigate *Gloire* from the French navy. North failed in his mission, and ultimately proved incompetent in most of his subsequent assignments. Fortunately for Mallory, Bulloch was more than capable of handling the Confederate navy's European operations on his own.

In the meantime, the first meaningful Confederate armed response to the blockade came from the CSS *Sumter*, a converted packet ship armed with an 8-inch swivel gun and four 32-pounders. Her captain was Commander Raphael Semmes, a highly experienced former United States Navy officer from Maryland. Nicknamed "Old Mustache Wax" by his crew, the raffish Semmes would later achieve international fame as the captain of the CSS *Alabama*.

Sumter departed from New Orleans on June 18, and over the next seven months the raider caused considerable distress to Northern mercantile shipping, taking seventeen prizes and burning seven ships before being bottled up by the United States Navy at Gibraltar in January 1862.

By August, Bulloch was in England with £131,000 to begin the purchase or construction of the Confederate ships, and over the next four years he became one of the key Confederate purchasing agents in England. His efforts to buy and arrange shipping for military supplies of all kinds, and to buy the most modern warships of the time, constantly bedeviled United States authorities.

Regarded by his contemporaries as an excellent man for the job, Bulloch descended from a family that settled in Georgia in 1729. His grandfather served in the Revolutionary War, and his father had become a wealthy landowner in Savannah. Bulloch himself served for a number of years as an officer in the United States Navy, but slow peacetime promotion eventually forced him to leave the service. He became a captain in a commercial maritime firm in New York City, resigning that position to become an officer in the Confederate navy when war broke out.

As a result of his efforts in England, *Sumter* was followed by even more successful English-built raiders for Confederate navy. The most effective was the feared *Alabama* which took 69 prizes, and the other raiders *Shenandoah* (48 prizes), *Tallahassee* (39 prizes), and *Florida* (36 prizes).

By the end of 1863, Confederate raiders had captured about 150 United States ships whose cargoes totaled about $13 million. Those captures forced commercial marine insurance rates to skyrocket, and eventually caused 385 United States merchant ships to be reflagged to foreign ownership. That was a disastrous blow with long-term effects upon the United States carrying trade; for the next fifty years most American transatlantic commerce would be carried in European ships with European crews.

The United States blockading fleet grew to 160 ships by the end of 1861, and real shortages of all kinds began to be felt in the South. There was even a shortage of Bibles, the majority of which were printed in the North and had been quickly declared as contraband of war. Wishing to have Bibles to distribute throughout the army, in August 1862 the Confederate Bible Society wrote to the British and Foreign Bible Society. They sought a £1,000 line of credit toward the cost of obtaining the books in England, mentioning that for the time being they could only pay interest on the credit.

The British Society responded with an initial interest-free loan of £3,000, and immediately forwarded the Bibles to Fraser, Trenholm & Co., a Liverpool shipping company, for delivery into the South.[6] Included with the implements of war, Fraser, Trenholm ultimately exported more than 300,000 Bibles, New Testaments and other religious materials for Confederate soldiers.

The ability to run a wide range of supplies through the blockade encouraged the Confederate commissioners in Europe. They wrote to Lord John Russell, British Secretary of State for Foreign Affairs, saying that despite the blockade more than four hundred blockade runners had passed safely through it. Without success, they urged British recognition based upon the seemingly obvious fact that the blockade had not prevented foreign access to the South and its supply of cotton.

CHAPTER THREE

Organizing International Supply Operations

EVEN before Fort Sumter was fired upon, Confederate authorities realized that not only did military supplies have to be obtained in quantity from abroad, but arrangements also had to be made to finance and ship them. Thus, in early April 1861 a committee of Charleston businessmen was appointed to look into establishing a Charleston-Liverpool steamship line to replace the Northern steamers that would no longer be in service. Because of its expertise and the connections of its principal owner, the obvious choice to handle overseas finance and shipping for the government was the firm of John Fraser & Company.

Founded in Charleston in 1803, John Fraser & Co. had developed into a powerful, respected trading and finance firm, known for its astute handling of import/export and financial matters for Southern planters and businessmen. By 1860 the growing firm had also established regular commercial service between Charleston and Liverpool using their own five ships. Two closely-linked subsidiaries, Trenholm Brothers in New York City and Fraser, Trenholm & Company in Liverpool, gave the firm an international presence. The Liverpool branch enjoyed a particularly good reputation within English banking and financial circles.

When war broke out, the New York branch was closed and reestablished in Nassau to work there with the local firm of Adderly & Company, while another branch was established in Bermuda. Those offices in Charleston, Liverpool, and the islands would later prove to be among the Confederacy's most valuable outposts. The firm effectively became, in the words of one observer, a "...member in absentia of the Southern cabinet."[1]

11

The firm's senior partner, George Alfred Trenholm, descended from an English family which had settled in Charleston in 1764. Supporters of King George III, they had been forced to leave the country for a while after the Revolution. However, the family was soon able to return to Charleston, where they quickly reestablished themselves among the city's commercial and social elite.

Young Trenholm joined John Fraser & Co. as a clerk, but his impeccable social credentials and shrewd business sense led to a meteoric career in the prosperous business. As an adult, he was widely thought to be the wealthiest man in the South, and his prewar personal investments in a broad range of industries had brought him into contact with some of the most powerful and prominent men in the United States and Europe.

Intelligent as well as patrician, one of Trenholm's first recommendations for the Confederate government was for it to buy ten first-rate ships that had been offered for sale by the British East India Company for $10 million. Richmond officials, however, failed to act upon the idea. Had they done so, the early problems of shipping large quantities through the blockade would have been greatly alleviated. [2]

By late Spring 1861, the government funded Fraser, Trenholm & Co. with $500,000 to commence European operations.[3] In general, they were to accept deposits of specie sent overseas by the government, handle the purchasing agents' letters of credit abroad, arrange the shipping of purchased supplies, and to act as overall clearing agent for the shipment and disbursement of cotton in Europe.

Procedurally, the Confederate government deposited its store of cash and bonds with John Fraser & Co. in Charleston, which in turn provided letters of credit upon those funds to Fraser, Trenholm & Co. in Liverpool. Fraser, Trenholm then issued the drafts actually used to pay for the purchases made by the Confederate agents in England.

The arrangement provided working capital for the agents in England, while at the same time allowing the Confederate government's limited amount of specie to remain in the South. For their services, John Fraser was permitted to charge a 1.5 percent commission on orders it handled for the government, the same fee it was believed the London banking firm of Baring Brothers earned for its similar services for the United States government. As well, the Trenholm firm earned fees for transporting government cargoes on their ships, and they were free to continue transacting business for their own account.

Over the course of the war Trenholm and his company earned a reputation for selfless patriotism toward the Southern cause. They unfailingly offered their transatlantic network of expertise, ships, and money whenever needed. Quite likely, the Confederate government's foreign supply program simply could not have existed without Trenholm. He and his partners of course made substantial profits for themselves from their activities,[4] but much of those profits were patriotically reinvested back into Confederate government securities.

That same month, the Confederate Ordnance Bureau, which was to play a pivotal role in foreign supply operations, was established under the command of highly-talented ordnance specialist Major (later Brigadier General) Josiah Gorgas.

Forty-three-year-old Gorgas had been born in Running Pumps, Lancaster County, Pennsylvania. After graduating from West Point he served in the Mexican War, and then in a number of assignments at various Ordnance posts. While at the Mount Vernon Arsenal in Alabama, he met and married Amelia Gayle, the daughter of the former governor of Alabama.

Completely sympathetic to the South by inclination and marriage, Gorgas resigned his captain's commission in the United States army in early April 1861. Recommended for the position by General P. G. T. Beauregard, sixteen days later Gorgas accepted the offer to be Chief of the Bureau of Ordnance and, temporarily, Acting Chief of the Engineer Bureau.

His first job was to equip what was estimated to be a 100,000-man Confederate army. However, because domestic supplies were inadequate for the job, he ordered Captain Caleb Huse to Europe to buy, at his discretion, whatever was needed and available, and to arrange for the shipping. At the beginning, Gorgas and Huse were in essence the entire Confederate foreign purchase department.

Like Gorgas, Huse was also a Yankee. Born in Massachusetts, at age twenty he graduated seventh in the West Point class of 1851. After one year of service as an artillery officer he married Harriet Pinckney, a Southern woman, and returned to West Point. There, he taught chemistry, geology, and mineralogy, and came to know Superintendent Robert E. Lee, a man he admired greatly. In 1859 he was assigned six months duty in Europe to study the European arms manufacturing industry and its dealers—knowledge that would later be invaluable to the Confederacy.

Upon his return he took a leave of absence from military duties to become superintendent at the University of Alabama. Preferring to remain in the South, Huse resigned his commission in February 1861, shortly before he was due to report back for active duty with the United States army. Instead, he accepted a commission in the Confederate army.

In April, Huse went to the Confederate capital at Montgomery, Alabama, where he was given rather ambiguous orders to go to England and buy ten thousand rifles and a battery of artillery.[5] However, since the government was unable to provide either money or sailing arrangements for his mission, his first task was to go to New York City where he was told that a bank there with Southern connections would give him letters of credit that the Trenholm Brothers office would convert into money for his trip.

He left Montgomery in mid-April, fearful that once in the North he would be discovered by United States army officers who knew him.[6] Taking a circuitous route through Charleston and Baltimore, in York, Pennsylvania, he boarded an empty Union troop train to Philadelphia. From there he traveled to South Amboy, New Jersey, and took a ferry to New York City.

Huse arrived at the bank just after a large body of soldiers troops had paraded down Broadway. Neither the expected cash nor the letters of credit were available, and one of the bankers suggested he call upon the Trenholm Brothers office for assistance. Although not expecting him, and preoccupied with their own safety, the Trenholm office managed to provide $500 in travel money. One of the understandably nervous partners urged him to arrange his passage to England from Canada, saying that New York was not a safe place for a Confederate agent: "The excitement is very great and if the crowds discover who you are they will hang you from a lamp post."

After several narrow escapes avoiding Union officers who knew him, Huse managed to board a ship for Liverpool, arriving there on May 10, 1861. He was joined a few weeks later by James Dunwoody Bulloch, and for the next four years the two men had the direct responsibility in Europe for obtaining, financing, and shipping much of the vast quantities of arms, ships, and other supplies needed by the Confederate government.

CHAPTER FOUR
The Pipeline Fills

UPON arriving in Liverpool, Huse went directly to London and booked a room in Morley's Hotel on Trafalgar Square. It was popular with Americans traveling on business, and was also conveniently located to both the offices of the British government at Whitehall and the London Armoury Company at 36 King William Street. Not far away was the Armoury Company's factory.

Huse immediately called at the Fraser, Trenholm office, and found to his dismay that only £10,000 was available to him to buy arms, although he got the firm's assurance of doing everything possible to assist him. As well, he learned that the remaining available supply of small arms was insignificant because Northern agents had arrived in England earlier and had been buying all the weapons they could find.

He visited the London Armoury Company the next day and promptly ran into a man he had known in Massachusetts, who was now an agent trying to buy arms for the United States government. Huse admitted bluntly that he "...was buying for the Confederate Government," and resolved to himself to try and "outflank" the U.S. agent's mission.

Founded in 1856, the privately-owned and pro-Southern London Armoury Company was sought after by both agents because it was the largest of the various manufacturers of the Model 1853 Enfield rifle-musket, the standard British army long arm. The modern weapon featured interchangeable parts, and in Huse's opinion the company's craftsmanship was "in every respect...equal to the Government works at Enfield."[1]

Huse asked superintendent Robert Adams to sell him the factory's output for three years, but the board of directors had to decline the order because of its previous commitment to the Northern agent. The company had already contracted to supply the United States government with one hundred Enfields per week for the next three months, with the balance of their total monthly production of thirteen hundred rifles going to the British government.[2]

However, exercising the initiative he was to become known for, Huse at once ordered ten thousand rifle-muskets of the current pattern, complete with bayonets, bayonet scabbards, extra nipples, snap caps, and tompions for a price per set of £3 16s. 9d (about $19.50) fob London. The company accepted that order, to be filled as soon as they completed their outstanding orders for other customers, with the proviso that a £15,000 deposit was required in case the order was canceled.[3] At Huse's request, the contract specified that he would also be the "preferred purchaser" for an additional 6,000 to 10,000 muskets.

That was the beginning of a long-standing relationship between the Armoury and the Confederacy. According to Huse, for the rest of the war the London Armoury Company "turned all its output of arms over to me for the Confederate Army," and the company became a quasi-official supplier to the Confederacy. In addition to Enfield rifle-muskets, the company also made the highly-prized .44 caliber Kerr five-shot revolver, some nine thousand of which were sent to the South during the war.

Needing more weapons than the London Armoury Company was able to supply, Huse also entered into a business relationship with one of their directors, Archibald Hamilton. A small-arms expert in his own right, Hamilton assisted Huse in finding and buying Enfields from among the other qualified manufacturers in the area. An initial $100,000 was deposited to the account of Sinclair, Hamilton & Company for the purchases, with Hamilton receiving a 2.5 percent commission on arms purchased through his efforts.

However, despite his obvious successes in obtaining equipment upon his arrival, some in the Confederate government questioned Huse's patriotism. He was, after all, a Yankee, and not widely known to many of those in the government at that early point.

Therefore, on orders from Jefferson Davis, Major Edward C. Anderson was dispatched to England in June to observe Huse's activities and to either replace him if necessary or to cooperate with and assist him with purchase operations. A wealthy planter, businessman, former United States Navy officer, and twice mayor of Savannah, Anderson sailed to England aboard the racing yacht *America*.[4] Once there, he quickly found that Huse was more than capable in his dealings, and that his loyalty was beyond reproach.

Anderson was thus free to concentrate on working with the other agents beginning to arrive in Europe. He had orders from Secretary of

War James A. Seddon to take control over Confederate purchasing operations in Europe, and to effectively become, in Seddon's words, "...the Secretary of War in England."

Anderson, Bulloch and Huse were at that time living together in a London apartment at 58 Jermyn Street, which the three arms specialists nicknamed "The Casemate." They began to use local British commercial agents to obtain the supplies they needed, and scoured the smaller workshops for arms and equipment to augment the production of the larger factories, most of which were running at maximum capacity.

As one of the largest customers in the English arms market, Huse received the usual small courtesies from his contractors and suppliers. These included such things as theatre tickets and "return commissions." These were small rebates, a typical English business custom of the day, which Huse used to offset his living expenses in England and to acquire a technical library for the Ordnance Bureau. Those rebates, however, would be misrepresented by several other officers in a later attempt to discredit Huse.

The Confederate agents in England worked with a number of local contractors on a commission basis to obtain the supplies they needed. The main contractor for army supplies was S. Isaac, Campbell & Company of London, another pro-Southern firm with whom Huse apparently made contact shortly after his arrival in England.

Experienced and seemingly well-connected as both a manufacturer[5] and contractor within the British military supply industry, the company also had a somewhat checkered reputation. While engaged as a contractor to the British army during the Crimean War, a company executive's loan of £500 to an army officer led to an investigation on bribery charges. The firm was acquitted of any wrongdoing, but its military contracts were canceled and they did very little business with the British army after that time.

Their reputation would later cause problems for Huse, but for several years S. Isaac, Campbell was a diligent servant of the Confederate government, not only as a prime contractor but as a company which often advanced its own funds to pay for the much-needed supplies. The company quickly became so intertwined with Confederate government orders and finance that in March 1862 Secretary of War Seddon thanked them "for the kind and generous confidence which you have exhibited toward us at a moment when all others in foreign countries seem to be doubtful, timorous, and wavering."

S. Isaac, Campbell offered Huse the advantages of one-stop shopping and good prices on bulk orders. Directly or indirectly, the firm would supply Huse with much of the buttons, belts and buckles, canteens, cartridge and cap pouches, swords, knapsacks, shoes, uniforms and bulk uniform cloth that he imported through 1864. Huse would certainly have had great difficulty in accomplishing his work without the services of the company, and it was no exaggeration when one of the senior partners said that the Confederacy owed everything to the willingness of the firm to equip their soldiers.

President Davis was so pleased with Huse's success and his use of initiative to act beyond orders when circumstances required, that in June 1861 he sent extraordinary orders telling him to move rapidly to acquire arms as he saw fit, and to act upon his own responsibility and not be controlled by other government agents.

In August, Anderson obtained the services of the "Tower Viewer," a trained British arms inspector who carefully reviewed the quality of the arms the agents were buying. That month alone, the agents bought ten thousand "old army pattern" rifle-muskets and twelve thousand smoothbore "Genoese muskets" through S. Isaac, Campbell.

Bulloch was also buying various small arms for the Confederate navy, his first orders being to acquire 1,000 Kerr-pattern navy revolvers and 1,000 navy carbines together with 100,000 rounds of ammunition and 500,000 percussion caps for each type of weapon. He also obtained 1,000 cutlasses and a variety of bullet moulds, gun wipers, and shoes.[6]

CHAPTER FIVE
The View From England

ENGLISH merchants could, and did, sell arms and equipment to both North and South, but the friendly reception Huse and the other agents encountered was no accident; sympathy for the Confederacy was widespread in England.

Certainly, the idea of slavery was distasteful in general, but English attitudes toward the South were formed along class lines. The working class tended to align its views with the Union, seeing in the American Civil War a struggle between free, egalitarian laborers in the North fighting against a South that sought to preserve a structured society headed by a landed aristocracy.

By contrast, the English middle and upper classes saw in the South a genteel, romantic way of life threatened by industrial vandals. That view was reinforced by the many commercial and blood ties between England and the South: England took the bulk of Southern cotton while the South received a steady stream of English goods, and Southern families often maintained links with their English roots.

As well, the British government and aristocracy had considerable resentment toward the growing economic and political power of the United States as represented by the North: *"an arrogant and encroaching people,"* in the words of Lord Westbury, the Lord Chancellor.[1] His thoughts reflected the opinion of England's ruling classes, which had no interest in preserving a united America against a Confederacy that "most resembled the Mother Country."

In supporting the South, England saw its chance, as Henry Steele Commager put it, to "humiliate" the upstart United States and its despised democratic practices.[2] But those in control of the government had to question whether British foreign policy was to be determined solely by the wishes of the upper classes. As well, England wanted to avoid becoming enmeshed in the war, yet wished—in fact almost needed—to continue trading with the Confederacy and with the North.

Both North and South initiated a propaganda war in England, seeking to increase their spheres of influence in that country. However, the influence of the Establishment was considerable in nineteenth-century England, and the major English newspapers and magazines came out on the side of the South, and the Church of England and the universities were also sympathetic.

Both sides also had local supporters in groups formed just for that purpose. For the North there were the various "Emancipation" Societies, while the South had its "Southern Independence Association." Again, however, the South garnered the greatest influence. Its powerful supporters included businessmen, manufacturers, politicians, and members of the peerage, whose considerable resources were used to help further the Southern cause in England.

North and South alike utilized journalism to a great degree, with the North's propaganda efforts focused upon using American reporters to produce American-style newspapers in England. Those newspapers, however, were no match for the brilliant Henry Hotze and his *Index.* Swiss-born, the twenty-seven-year-old Hotze had previously served on the editorial staff of the *Mobile Register,* and he wisely perceived that Northern propagandists with their "nasal twang and aggressiveness" would be "most repulsive to English taste." [3]

Sent to England and financed by the Confederate government, he decided to produce an English-style newspaper written for the most part by local English reporters and writers. Named the *Index,* it described itself as a "Weekly Journal of Politics, Literature and News," and indeed it covered areas of wide interest to its sophisticated readership.

But the paper also constantly reminded its readers of the "non-British" character of the North with statements such as "The South for generations back had been prouder of its closer affinity of blood to the British parental stock than the North with its mongrel compound of the surplus population of the world."

The *Index* was a major success. From its first issue on May 1, 1862, and throughout the war, the erudite newspaper became must-reading for members of the British government, intelligentsia, and upper classes. The paper's wide readership included subscribers throughout Europe and even some in the North, and Hotze's efforts clearly did much to aid the agents in their work.

While the propagandists were at work, more pressing problems had to be addressed: whether England would grant recognition to the Confederacy as a nation, and whether English firms could sell arms and equipment to both sides. The latter was particularly important to the Confederacy, which depended upon the flow of those goods.

England had granted the rights of a belligerent nation to the Confederacy, but those rights were carefully circumscribed. Southern agents, Bulloch in particular, still had to carefully operate within the scope of Britain's Neutrality Law of April 20, 1818. Better known as the *Foreign Enlistment Act*, it governed the actions of a neutral Britain toward belligerent nations.

As to Bulloch and his ambitious orders to acquire a navy, the Act's key points were: 1. a belligerent's ships could dock in British ports, but could take on only enough coal to reach the nearest home port; 2. no such ships could mount guns in Britain or increase their existing armament; 3. British citizens were prohibited from enlisting or serving in a belligerent's armed forces.

To reinforce the government's position, on May 15, 1861, *The Queen's Proclamation of Neutrality* was issued, and announced to the world that Britain's role would be to "observe a strict neutrality" in the conflict. The rapid issuance of the Proclamation the day of the arrival of United States Minister Charles Adams led some in the North to perceive a certain British unfriendliness toward the Union.

Nevertheless, no sooner was Queen Victoria's signature dry on the document than Confederate agents, led by Bulloch and with the assistance of English legal experts and private shipbuilders, began to utilize loopholes in the law. Bulloch interpreted the laws to mean that there was no violation of them even if certain ships that looked warlike were built by or sold to presumably innocent purchasers, nor if those ships were subsequently armed and manned offshore.

Neither was it a violation, he contended, if a British-registered ship sailed from an English port carrying a cargo of naval guns and supplies, even if that ship eventually joined the unarmed other ship and transferred its cargo of weapons to her. These in fact became exactly the methods Bulloch used to buy and equip the Confederate commerce raiders.

At the same time, Charles Adams had set up an excellent intelligence network which constantly spied on the clandestine activities of the Confederate agents. Adams was particularly concerned with developments in Bulloch's naval and transport activities, and he used his information to constantly pressure the British government to bring a halt to Confederate endeavors. His letter of August 15, 1861, to Lord John Russell, Britain's Foreign Secretary, is typical:

> My Lord: It is stated to me that a new screw steamer called the Bermuda, ostensibly owned by the commercial house of Fraser, Trenholm & Co., of Liverpool, well known to consist in part of Americans in sympathy with the insurgents in the United States, is now lying at West Hartlepool, ready for sea. She is stated to carry English colors but to be commanded by a

Frenchman...This steamer is armed with four guns, and she has been for some time taking in crates, cases, and barrels, believed to contain arms and munitions of all kinds ordinarily used in carrying on war. The cargo is nominally entered for Cuba, but her armament and cargo are of such a nature as to render it morally certain that the merchants who claim to be the owners can have no intention of dispatching her on any errand of mercy or peace.[4]

English acquiescence to such a loose interpretation of their own laws—"friendly neutrality" in the words of Fitzgerald Ross—[5] infuriated Adams, and Bulloch's easy access to the latest in Royal Navy weapons technology later brought England and the United States to the brink of war. To frustrate Adams and his intelligence service, Bulloch constantly engaged in a devilish cat-and-mouse game to disguise the true owners, cargoes and purposes of his ships in England. The case of the English merchant ship *Sea-King* was typical.

In September 1864 the *Sea-King* was "sold" to a man who coincidentally was also the father-in-law of the man in charge of the Fraser, Trenholm office. The following month the new owner authorized another Englishman to sell the ship within six months, but the next *day* the ship sailed away and was "sold" again on the high seas to Confederate buyers. A few days later the *Sea-King* was met off the coast of Madeira by an English tender that brought cannon, munitions, and about one hundred crewmen. Within a few hours they transformed the harmless merchant ship into the raider *Shenandoah*.

Despite the fact that the United States also bought large quantities of supplies in England without any interference from the British government, Britain's announced neutrality but apparent partiality to the South became a source of great anguish for the United States government during the war. While the South would become frustrated and eventually bitter over Britain's failure to grant political recognition, it was the North that suffered actual losses of men and ships from British-supplied arms and ships used by the Confederates.

To prove its point, after the war the United States government sued Britain in international court. The grounds alleged were that the British government was completely aware of the military purposes of the ships acquired by Bulloch, and that British tenders that supplied the Confederate ships were in violation of the letter and spirit of British neutrality.

After considerable testimony in what became known as the "Alabama Claims," one of the most famous cases in international law, the United States was awarded some $16 million in damages from the British government.

ILLUSTRATIONS

Library of Congress

George Alfred Trenholm

24

Library of Congress

Col. Josiah Gorgas, Chief of Ordnance, C.S.A.
His nose was broken in a childhood accident when he tripped over his
father's leg.

The Supplies for the Confederate Army

Capt. Caleb Huse, C.S.A. in later life.

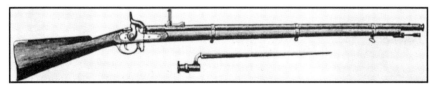

Catalogue: Schuyler, Hartley and Graham

The preferred Confederate army long arm: a British army M1853 "Enfield" 0.577 calibre rifle-musket with its bayonet. Fifty-five inches in length and weighing about nine pounds, it was accurate to more than 1,000 yards.

Inwards.

Port of

IN the Ship *Bermuda* British Built, Property all British about 716 Tons, with 40 Men, besides C. M. Man, Master for this present Voyage from *Liverpool.*

(handwritten cargo manifest — multiple columns of marks, numbers, and goods including cases of leather, haberdashery, saddlery, hosiery, millinery, stationery, woollens, cottons, drugs, hardware, shoes, porcelain, perfumery, cards, teasels, bichrome, wool braid, needles, knives, surgical instruments, shot, soap, paper, sheeting, kid gloves, printing, etc.)

I DO swear, that this entry now tendered and subscribed by me, is a just report of the name of the above-mentioned Ship, its burthen, built, property, number, and country of mariners, the present master and voyage: And that it further contains a true account of the lading of the said Ship, with, the particular marks, numbers, quantity, quality, and consignment of all the goods and merchandizes in the said Ship, to the best of my knowledge and belief; and that bulk hath not been broke, nor any goods delivered out of the said Ship since her loading in

So help me GOD.

Sworn before Us, the   Day of

Bermuda Archives

The *Bermuda's* extensive manifest from a voyage in early 1862. The valuable cargo of military and civilian goods was lost to the South when the ship was captured off the Bahama Islands by the United States Navy.

Continued

Inwards   Steamer *Bermuda*

Port of   IN the Ship *Bermuda*
Built, Property all   about
Tons, with   Men,

Men,
a

this present Voyage from   besides
Man, Master for

2 Cases Woollens   1 Case print Materials   250 Cases Shell
5 do Cottons   1 Package do   2 Cases Copper Tubes
10 " Cotton Thread   2 Case do
13 " Cotton   10 Cases do   1 Cannon (loose)
8 " Woollen   20 - - Paper   100 Cases Shell
53 " Cottons   1 - - Ink   120 - - - Do
3 - Hardware Buttons   1 - Machinery   18 - - - - Do
15 - Paper   9 - Print Materials   41 - - - - do
1 Linen Thread   14 Ingots Block Tin   1 Case Fuses
2 Bales Woollens   16 Cases Stationery   1 - Furniture
5 - " Blankets   12 - " Print Materials   2 Cases Gun Carriage
2 - "   y Cases Pistols   4
16 Boxes Linen Thread   208 Coils Manilla Rope   3 Cases
70 Bales Woollens   240 Cases Tools   Machine
2 do Blankets   12 Leggings
38 - - - "   64 Bales Hides   1 Cannon (Loose)
1 - - Woollens   1723 Sides Leather   1 - -
20 - Blankets   250 - "   7 Field Carriages
6 Cases Military Caps   1200 Boxes Glass   2 Limbers
5 Drums Sewing Cable   10 Chest Tea   2 Bundles Poles &c
1 Box Joiners Tools   20 Boxes - Do   2 Cases Cannon
1 Bale Woollens   6 Half Chests - Do   2 - " -
4 Cases Shoe Thread   25 Boxes - Do   14 - Swords
1 Cask Hardware   4 Half Chests   3 - Do
6 Cases Guns   84 Bags Coffee   Do
3 Cases Hardware   122 - Do -   70 Bbls Cartridges
2 Casks "   32 - Do - Do -
1 Case "   6 - - - Do -   300 Bbls Gun Powder
3 Casks "   25 - Do -   76 Half Bbls "
4 Cases Steel   712 Bags Salt Petre   177 Qr "
1 Case Hardware   3 Barrels Bar Tin   470 - - - "
24 Bundles Shades   5 - - - Ingots   2 Half Bbls do
3 Rolls Wire Cloth   28 Ingots -   6 Qr - - - "
2 Bales Bags   35 Pkgs Lead   47 Cases Merchandize
1 Roll Wire Cloth   35 - - Sheet -   5 Bales - "
1 Cask Hardware   200 Bars Tin Plates
1 Box - Do   100 do Tomb Plates   1 Case - "
2 " Cotton Thread   10 Bundles Iron Wire   1 Box - "
2 Trusses Haberdashery   3 Cases Cannon
4 Hhds Hose Swing   1 - - - Do -   7 Cases - "
10 Bales Oakum   1 - - - Carriage
2 Coils Rope   60 - - Shell
4 Coils do Hawsers   20 - - Do

I DO swear, that this entry now tendered and subscribed by me, is a just report of the
name of the above-mentioned Ship, its burthen, built, property, number, and country
of mariners, the present master and voyage: And that it further contains a true account
of the luding of the said Ship, with the particular marks, numbers, quantity, quality,
and consignment of all the goods and merchandizes in the said Ship, to the best of my
knowledge and belief; and that bulk hath not been broke, nor any goods delivered out
of the said Ship since her loading in

So help me GOD.

Sworn before Us
the 24 Day of Mar 1862

Battles and Leaders of the Civil War
Commander James Dunwoody Bulloch, C.S.N.

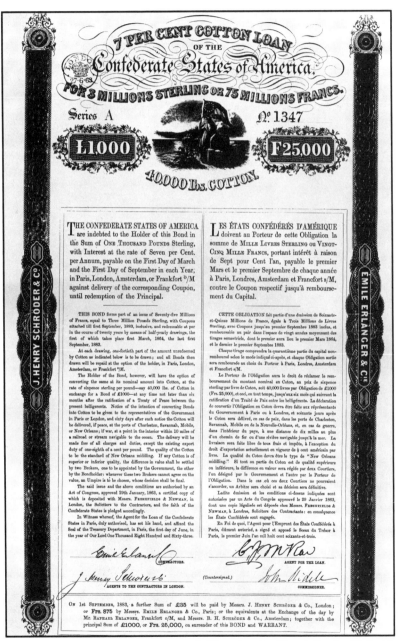

By permission, S. Waite Rawls, III and Charles W. Smithson
The Evolution of Risk management Products

An Erlanger Certificate, denominated in both Sterling and Francs and convertible into cotton.

30

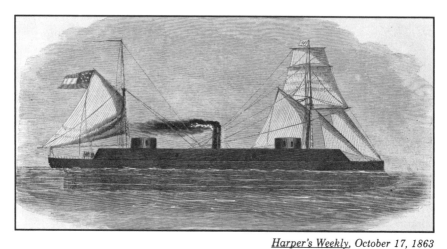

Harper's Weekly, October 17, 1863

One of the Laird Rams, described by the magazine as an "Anglo-Rebel Pirate."

Courtesy of the North Carolina Division of Archives and History

The blockade runner *Hope*. Built in England for Fraser, Trenholm & Co. in 1864, her cargo capacity was triple that of most other blockade runners. She is shown here being captured off Wilmington by the USS *Eolus* in October 1864.

Library of Congress

Stephen R. Mallory
Secretary of the Confederate States Navy
Intelligent and well-connected in Richmond society, Mallory was one
of just two members of the cabinet to serve throughout the war.

Cape Fear Museum

The *Col. Lamb*, sister ship to the *Hope*. Named in honor of William Lamb, the commander of Fort Fisher, the ship avoided capture and returned to England after the war.

Weighing Cotton on Compress Docks.

Cape Fear Museum

The cotton compresses on the docks at Wilmington could pack about five hundred pounds of cotton fiber into one bale for ease of shipment.

Harper's Weekly

Blockade runners *Nashville* and *Tuscarora* docked at Southampton, England. The *Tuscarora* was owned for a while in 1862 by John Fraser & Co. Renamed the *Thomas L. Wragg* and later the *Rattlesnake*, she was destroyed by the United States Navy in February 1863.

Harper's Weekly

Flying the Stars and Bars, a Confederate blockade runner enters the harbor at Nassau.

"No. 294," also known as *El Tousson*, was the first of the two Laird rams to be completed. Bulloch devised a scheme to have a French banking house purchase the rams ostensibly for the Egyptian navy. Once at sea, they were to be transferred to Confederate ownership. The plan failed when Adams threatened war with England.

Courtesy of the North Carolina Division of Archives and History

Fort Fisher shortly after its fall to United States forces. Located some eighteen miles down river from Wilmington, the "Gibraltar of the South" guarded the entrance to the Cape Fear River. Among its armament were English-made artillery pieces, including an Armstrong rifled cannon capable of firing 150-pound shells.

Fort Fisher, commanding the new inlet entrance to Cape Fear River. The British steamer *Hansa* running the blockade under the guns of the fort.

Harper's Weekly

Confederate ironclad rams engage United States blockade ships off Charleston in January 1863.

Harper's Weekly

England's "friendly neutrality" toward the South was a frequent subject of cartoons in Northern magazines. Here, John Bull (England) is shown as a shopkeeper gladly selling arms and ships ("290" is a Laird ram) to Jefferson Davis. The caption reads: "All right, Mr. Confederate—the money's all right. Call at our little shop again, Sir. Fit you out as a Pirate, or make you Manacles for slaves at shortest notice."

A sarcastic view of the North ("Brother Jonathan") coming to the aid
of English mill workers starving because of the lack of Southern cotton.

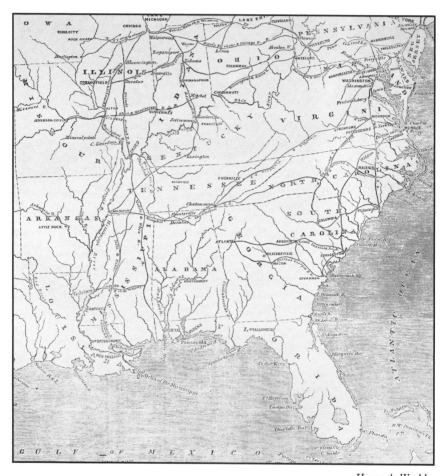

Harper's Weekly

Map showing the line of the blockade, and the strategic routes in the interior. The huge length of the Southern coast made it difficult at first for theUnion navy to maintain an effective blockade.

Harper's Weekly

Charleston, South Carolina, and its harbor in early 1861.

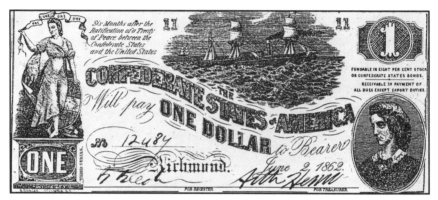

Author's Collection

The steamship shown on this Confederate $1 dollar bill of 1862 conveys the importance of foreign commerce to the South.

Harper's Weekly

Jefferson Davis' optimistic speeches to the contrary, by late 1862 Confederate government finances continued to weaken.

James Mason and John Slidell were the Confederate commissioners to England and France. They were feared and ridiculed by the Northern press because of their considerable involvement with foreign governments.

Built in Liverpool for Bulloch under the guise of an Italian commercial ship, the *Oreto* sailed to the Bahamas where despite protests from the United States consul she received her armament. Renamed the *Florida*, the ship had a successful career as a privateer. In an embarrassing moment for the United States Navy, shown above, the *Florida* dashes safely out of Mobile Bay through a waiting squadron of blockade ships.

Author's Collection

A British musket cap pouch bearing the stamp of S. Isaac, Campbell & Co. Variations of the company's stamp were impressed or stenciled on the items they provided to the Confederacy.

Philip Katcher Collection

Large quantities of British army wooden canteens were exported to the Confederacy. They were painted light blue and bore the "broad arrow" mark of the British government. Although they held considerably more water than American military canteens, their larger size and weight made them somewhat uncomfortable to carry in the field.

Catalogue: Francis Bannerman Sons

A British military knapsack, typical of those Huse and the other agents exported in large quantities. This version was made of waterproofed black linen with tanned leather straps. A coat or blanket could be secured in the loops on top. In the late 1920s, military supply dealer Francis Bannerman Sons was selling the knapsacks as surplus for the incredible price of just $1.00.

Courtesy, Civil War Museum and Library of Philadelphia

The Union army also used some British equipment. Here, men of the 44th Massachusetts Infantry are shown equipped with British-made cap pouches, cartridge boxes, and Enfield rifles. Their waist belts are fitted with the common British "snake buckle." The equipment was taken from a captured Confederate blockade runner.

CHAPTER SIX

Arms and Controversy

BY early June 1861 Huse and Bulloch had made a number of purchases, and English warehouses were bursting with supplies they had ordered. Through September, Huse had received $1.4 million to buy arms and supplies for the Ordnance Bureau,[1] but the Queen's Proclamation of Neutrality and the presence of the United States Navy had prevented shipping the goods. In the meantime, Fraser, Trenholm had acquired three new ships, and in an effort to both get some of the supplies home and prove the ineffectiveness of the blockade, they decided to send one of their ships, the *Bermuda,* through the blockade.

Many other ships had already run the blockade, but they transported essentially civilian cargoes; the *Bermuda* was the first ship to leave England for the Confederate States with a cargo that was primarily military in nature.

Fraser, Trenholm's freight charges were steep, but it was Anderson's only way to send home some of the growing amount of supplies. The *Bermuda* arrived unchallenged in Savannah on September 28, carrying a mixed cargo of much-needed supplies. Aboard were 18 large rifled cannon, 4 seacoast guns complete with their carriages, powder and shot, 6,500 to 7,500 Enfield rifle-muskets, 18,000 Belgian rifles with fixed ammunition, 200,000 cartridges, 180 barrels of gunpowder, and a variety of medical supplies.[2] As well, the ship carried arms consigned to private individuals in the South who used them to equip certain units. One such man, Wade Hampton of South Carolina, obtained 200 short Enfields, 20,000 cartridges, and two 6-pounder guns.[3]

A month later, to the delight of English merchants, the *Bermuda* returned to Liverpool carrying a large supply of cotton.

46

That same month other shipments began of the Enfields acquired by Hamilton, and within several months Huse found himself under considerable pressure by also having to buy supplies for the Quartermaster, Medical, Navy and War departments. To add to the burden, Huse and Anderson were not only buying for an army which had grown from one hundred thousand men to more than a half million within months, but they were usually competing with United States and even foreign buyers for the same arms and equipment.

There was little margin for error in their dealings, because there never were more than 1,000 to 2,000 small arms in reserve in the Confederacy.[4] Competition to buy was feverish at this stage, and the arrival of government funds was critical in determining which side could obtain supplies in the market. British suppliers were requiring cash advances from both sides in case the war ended early.

By July 1861 neither side's agents had received any cash from their governments, and it was only by a stroke of luck that Huse and Anderson received their money first, enabling them to buy what Huse described as "a very superior lot of Enfield rifles that the United States first ordered."

Although United States agents usually had almost unlimited funds at their disposal and thus bought practically anything offered to them, Huse said they often bought "the merest rubbish in the world," in part to keep the weapons out of Confederate hands.

He also noted that the United States buying caused the prices for even worthless muskets to become "fabulous." He and Anderson remained selective in their purchases, preferring to buy Enfields whenever available, but otherwise only arms in good condition. Of the 131,129 long arms shipped by Huse as of March 1863, 81,049—62 percent—were Enfields.

At one point, the Confederates also thought of buying up all the small arms available in England and elsewhere in Europe, including poor-quality weapons, just to keep them out of the hands of the North. Huse rejected that suggestion, however, saying the old weapons would "prove more dangerous to those who may venture to use them than to the troops against whom they are pointed."

Indeed, those were almost the exact words used by Ulysses S. Grant after the war in describing the mixture of weapons used by United States troops in the west. By comparison, he noticed that Confederate soldiers in that theatre "had generally new arms, which had run the blockade, and were of uniform caliber."

The Missouri Brigade, among others, had obtained their new Enfields just several months before the fall of Vicksburg, and Grant was able to obtain a good supply of them for his own men when he authorized them to replace their muskets with the discarded Enfields of the surrendered Confederate soldiers.

The year 1861 also saw the arrival in the South of the largest load of armaments ever to come in one ship during the war. Leaving Greenock, Scotland on October 8, the *Fingal*, newly-purchased by Anderson and Bulloch and manned by a mostly British crew, carried into Savannah some 15,000 rifles (mostly Enfields), more than 2 million cartridges, 24,100 pounds of powder, 2 million percussion caps, 230 swords and 3,000 cavalry sabers, 500 revolvers with ammunition, 2 Blakely guns, 2 smaller cannon, 7 tons of artillery shells, 400 barrels of gunpowder, as well as blankets, medical supplies, and a huge amount of army and navy uniforms and uniform cloth.[5]

The *Fingal* was also important in that for the first time government supplies were brought in on a government-owned ship. Not only were freight costs drastically reduced, none of the cargo space had to be shared with the non-essential civilian items Fraser, Trenholm and other private owners of ships insisted on transporting. Heretofore, the superfluous but highly profitable civilian cargoes often took up more than two-thirds of a ship's cargo space, causing backlogs in shipping military supplies.

Anderson and Bulloch were also aboard the *Fingal*. Anderson thought his work was finished in Europe, and Bulloch, keenly aware that the government needed to have its own fleet of transport ships, was returning to discuss with Mallory the feasibility of building such ships in England and using cotton to pay for their construction.

By February 1862 the costs of Huse's purchases, shipping and insurance came to £249,853. 1s 0d. At the same time, other Confederate supplies in England awaiting shipment amounted to 23,000 rifles, 2,012,000 cartridges, and three million percussion caps. In Vienna another 30,000 rifles were ready for transport home. Total purchases through that date came to £1,186472. 19s 3d.[6] By February, the price to Huse for 50,000 Enfields had dropped to about $15.00 each, the same price being charged to the British army, although payment still had to be made in advance of delivery.

He continued buying at a strong pace, and in April reported that he was sending the *Minna* with 5,700 rifles, 5,900 knapsacks, 5,690 sets of accouterments, 1,840 gun slings, 1,850 sabers and 992 saber belts, 300 pairs of shoes, and 4,500 yards of light blue cloth.[7]

Even with shipping bottlenecks and delays, arms and supplies were getting through in increasing amounts. On August 16 Gorgas reported that Huse had obtained 48,150 "stand of arms" since April, and in a December letter to the secretary of war, Gorgas praised Huse's "rare forecast" in buying arms not on any list but which he knew would be needed. These included 157,000 stand of arms and other supplies that totaled $3,095,139.18, and Huse still needed another $5,925,402.08 to pay for supplies.[8]

All told, the Confederate War Department spent some $9 million on arms and equipment in fiscal 1861-1862. Generally speaking, throughout the war the combination of imports and local manufactures was sufficient to meet demands. The constant problem at home was in getting those supplies distributed to where the armies were located.

By the end of 1862 Huse had shipped large amounts of small arms, artillery, uniforms and uniform cloth, and such items as 16,178 cavalry sabers, 5,392 saber belts, 34,732 sets of accouterments, 40,240 rifle slings, 34,655 knapsacks, 4,000 canteen straps, 81,406 bayonet scabbards, and 650 sets of sergeants' accouterments. On his own initiative, he had used about $5 million of his $6 million line of credit to buy supplies, mostly from S. Isaac, Campbell, and much of it on credit advanced by them.

Because of delays in receiving funds, Huse owed them about $2 million, a large sum in those days, and the firm was pressing for payment. They said while they were willing to do everything to help the Confederacy, including replacing, within just three months, all the arms, uniforms, and equipment for one hundred thousand men lost when a blockade runner was captured, they were almost out of money because of prior advances to Huse. In a taste of what was to come in Confederate financing, the firm inquired about accepting some of the new cotton certificates they had heard about.

The Confederate agents in England had been working well as a group—Huse said he found them to be "cultured men, of agreeable personality."[9] It therefore came as a shock when vicious charges were leveled against Huse by Captain William G. Crenshaw in the winter of 1862–1863. Huse's reputation was temporarily damaged, but worse, the supply process was disrupted and S. Isaac, Campbell & Co. was ultimately ruined.

Crenshaw owned woolen and import/export businesses in Richmond, and managed to strike a unique bargain with the secretary of war. Under its terms, Crenshaw was to go to England and form a partnership with a British mercantile firm to obtain and ship supplies for the War and Navy departments. Ostensibly, this was to alleviate some of Huse's burden, although it was done without his knowledge. Crenshaw's partner was Alexander Collie, a respectable man who was a principal in a London shipping firm bearing his name.

The arrangement between the partners and the Confederate government was that the government would pay three-fourths the costs of building new transport ships, with Collie and Crenshaw paying the remainder. Half the cargo space aboard the new ships was to be allocated to the War Department, one-fourth to the Navy Department, with Collie and Crenshaw having the remaining fourth for their personal use.

Given the escalating values of civilian goods brought in to the South and of cotton taken back to England, the partners stood to make windfall profits far in excess of their contribution to building the ships. In addition, they were to receive a 2.5 percent commission on these or any other ships or supplies they purchased, and on any cotton they sold for the government.

Four new double-screw steamers, each worth about £14,500, were ordered for delivery in England between April and July 1863. Crenshaw then demanded of Huse that not only was he to provide ordnance and medical supplies, but that they were to be transported on the Collie-Crenshaw ships.

Huse dismissed the idea, saying that the government already owned four ships with a fifth under construction, and those ships would be idled if Collie-Crenshaw's ships were used. He further refused to sanction any purchasing by Collie-Crenshaw, except through S. Isaac, Campbell, a company Huse said was far more familiar with the intricacies of the arms and military supplies markets.

Huse pointed out that since S. Isaac, Campbell purchased much of the goods directly from the manufacturers, they could strike better bargains without the extra 2.5 percent commission the inexperienced Collie-Crenshaw partners were charging. Finally, Huse said that he would continue to handle all buying, as he was not prepared to "place the purchasing of the ordnance and medical supplies in your hands."

Crenshaw continued to barrage Huse with demands, including one for £115,334 in cash to help pay for the Collie-Crenshaw ships. Huse, who had been working feverishly to reduce the indebtedness of his own operations, refused to go along with any of Crenshaw's demands, believing that Crenshaw's real purpose was to monopolize all the government shipping business and fees for his company.

Frustrated and under pressure, Crenshaw wrote to Secretary of War Seddon, claiming that S. Isaac, Campbell was overcharging the government on purchases. He went on to impugn Huse's relationship with them, saying that he had accepted commissions from the firm. Major J. B. Ferguson, in London buying supplies for the quartermaster's department, joined in and wrote to the quartermaster-general, alleging that Huse had paid 50 percent over invoice for some supplies and received a 2.5 percent commission on some of them.

By mid-June, the situation had gotten to the point where it was affecting purchasing operations. Fortunately, Huse had powerful supporters who came to his defense. Among them was Josiah Gorgas, who wrote to the secretary of war saying that it was preposterous for anyone to even think that Huse, a professional military officer for fifteen years, would accept a commission or a bribe.

He pointed out that while Huse often did overpay 50 percent for some items, it was only because even at those prices the goods were cheaper than if bought at Confederate ports, and that Huse had actually saved the government millions, facts which Crenshaw and Ferguson simply weren't aware of.

It was decided to have an inquiry into the matter, and General Colin J. McRae, who was in Europe to head up the impending Erlanger Loan, was asked to have S. Isaac, Campbell's books audited. McRae had earned a substantial fortune before the war as an international cotton factor, and those dealings gave him some expertise in foreign financial matters. Even as his investigation began, McRae acknowledged the importance of S. Isaac, Campbell by saying "this house, which has been so maligned by our overzealous friends, is likely to be ruined by having trusted our Government when nobody else would."[10]

However, by July 1864 a London accounting firm found that S. Isaac, Campbell kept two sets of books and did indeed overcharge for supplies they bought. The relationship with the firm was severed, but Huse was personally absolved of all intentional error and malfeasance, and was complimented for his zeal and personal honor.

In defense of S. Isaac, Campbell & Co. it should be noted that they advanced large sums of their own money for government purchases, were patient in waiting for reimbursement, and accepted as payment various Confederate currency, securities, and cotton certificates, all of which fluctuated wildly in value.

Including overcharges, they still obtained more supplies at lower prices than most other firms in the business. They of course made profits, but that was hardly an unusual thing for any number of Southern or English companies involved in the trade. Even the renowned Trenholm companies shipped military supplies to Confederate ports where they auctioned or sold them to the highest bidder.

Of itself, the situation was symptomatic of the Confederacy's growing problem. There were too many agents, departments, and even states competing against each other for the same supplies, financing, and shipping. The elite Confederate Engineers, for example, sent their own agent, Captain John M. Robinson, to England for seven months to buy £12,000 worth of equipment that Huse probably could have bought for less and shipped home faster. The state of North Carolina went so far as to have its own blockade runner, the *Advance*,[11] which had a long and very successful career.

The government finally recognized the need to correct the problem, and McRae, an Alabamian with an excellent reputation and the knack to get along well with the agents, was appointed chief agent for all Confederate foreign purchase operations. He quickly sorted out the differences between Crenshaw and Huse, took control of overseas disbursements, and generally streamlined government purchase and shipping matters.

With funds in hand from the proceeds of the Erlanger Loan, Huse and the other agents were able to buy in quantity again. The size of Confederate imports in 1863 can be gauged by a United States government report made after the war, which estimated that for just *one week* in late 1863 260,000 pounds of supplies were imported.[12] During another period earlier in the year imports included 78,520 yards of cloth and 17,894 yards of flannel to be used for uniforms, 8,675 greatcoats, 8,250 pairs of trousers, and 6,703 shirts.

CHAPTER SEVEN
Government Finance and Control

BY the winter of 1862–1863 Confederate government finances were stretched to the limit for foreign purchasing. Through February 1863 Huse alone had brought in vast amounts of military supplies, including: 180,000 small arms (92 percent of them rifles), 129 cannon, over four million cartridges,[1] ten million percussion caps, 500,000 pounds of black powder, 16,178 cavalry sabers and 5,392 saber belts, 34,655 knapsacks, 34,731 sets of accouterments, 74,006 pairs of boots, 62,025 blankets, 8,675 greatcoats, 170,724 pairs of socks, and 78,520 yards of cloth.

He had spent some $5 million on supplies, only about half of which was covered by letters of credit backed in specie. Merchants in England were no longer receptive to accepting Confederate currency and securities which were becoming more devalued without the hard cash needed to back them. As well, the problem remained of having to deal with the owners of private ships to get the government's supplies shipped.

However, some relief came when the Ordnance Department finally began using its own steamers, the *Columbia, Eugenie, R. E. Lee*, and the *Merrimac*, to transport supplies from England. For the twelve-month period ending September 30, 1863, the ships brought in 113,504 small arms, almost four times as many as were manufactured in the domestic arsenals at Asheville, Fayetteville, and Richmond.

Total imports to that date included about 350,000 small arms, which included some 100,000 Austrian Lorenz rifles.[2] Huse, who had spent time as a military observer in Austria in 1859, quickly seized the opportunity offered when the Imperial Austrian Arsenal decided to replace their "rifles of the latest pattern..." and ten 6-gun batteries of artillery with weapons that used gun cotton instead of black powder.

With the shipping operation finally beginning to run smoothly, the government decided to begin financing foreign purchases with the one asset it had in abundance—cotton. Some 400,000 bales of cotton had been obtained by the government as pledges for its domestic Produce Loans. Furthermore, the withholding of that cotton from English mills—"King Cotton Diplomacy"—had failed to force political recognition from England. Richmond officials concluded that since prices for the commodity had skyrocketed in England, it made good economic sense to use the cotton as payment for imports.

Distribution was done by issuing "warrants" for cotton in bulk amounts.[3] The warrants appear to have been in bearer form, allowing the holders to take delivery of their cotton at Confederate ports. To make the proposition even more attractive, the cotton was priced at eight cents per pound, about one-quarter the price the commodity was trading for in London at the time.

The first certificates, in the amount of £62,000,[4] were secretly issued to several Europeans, with the proceeds used by the Confederate navy for its shipbuilding program. Word of the new certificates soon leaked out, however, and all the suppliers were eager to acquire bargain-priced cotton, the Confederacy's "White Gold," which could be converted into large profits.

S. Isaac, Campbell & Co. readily agreed to take them in exchange for debts owed by the government's agents in England, and about $1.5 million worth of certificates were then issued to Fraser, Trenholm, upon which Bulloch, Huse, and the other agents could draw for their purchases.

The availability of securitized cotton drew the attention of Erlanger & Company, a prominent French investment banking firm that had connections throughout Europe. They proposed underwriting a much larger issue of cotton-backed bonds to be distributed in England and Europe. After much negotiation with Confederate officials, it was decided that the bond issue, which became known as the "Erlanger Loan," would have a twenty-year maturity and pay annual interest at the rate of 7 percent.

However, the main attraction for investors was that the bonds could be exchanged into cotton at the bargain rate of sixpence (12¢) per pound, a price still well below its open-market value in England and Europe. The issue was in fact structured by the underwriters to pressure investors to convert into cotton, for a sinking fund was scheduled to begin one year after issue date. By its terms, every six months one-fortieth of the issue was to be randomly selected and redeemed at face value for cash.

Since the bonds were in bearer form, all bond holders risked the prospect of simply getting their principal back until they converted into cotton. Those who wished to convert would take physical delivery of their cotton at specified Southern ports if the Confederacy was at peace, otherwise "at points in the interior of the country within ten miles of a railroad or stream navigable to the ocean."

Confederate buying operations practically ceased during the months leading up to the sale of the bonds, with the agents spending most of their time trying to placate their suppliers with the promise of money to be available after the bonds were sold. McRae was appointed to be special agent in charge of handling the sale, and on March 19 the £3 million dual-currency (it was denominated in Sterling and Francs) issue was simultaneously offered in Amsterdam, Frankfurt, Liverpool, London, and Paris.

Wildly successful, within two days the Erlanger issue attracted £16 million in orders from a list of subscribers that included Chancellor of the Exchequer William Gladstone and a host of some of the most prominent and wealthy names in England.

Of the issue the London *Economist* remarked that "it may appear somewhat startling that the Confederates should be able to borrow in Europe while the Federal Government has been unable to obtain a shilling from that usually liberal and enterprising quarter." Erlanger's underwriting fees were extortionate and there were costs to maintain and service the sinking fund, but enough hard-currency proceeds[5] were available for the agents to settle long-overdue accounts with their contractors.

S. Isaac, Campbell took some cash and a large amount of the bonds in payment of money owed to them. Loyal to the end, as the bonds declined in value over the next year while they were being investigated, the company agreed to not dump them on the open market even though they were again hard-pressed for cash.

Most of the proceeds were directed for the use of Bulloch, to pay for the construction of two ironclad ships. A year earlier Bulloch had contracted for the Laird & Sons shipyard[6] at Birkenhead to build the two powerful ships, the so-called "Laird Rams," which incorporated the latest in Royal Navy weapons technology. Powered by steam and sail, and equipped with two revolving turrets each containing dual Whitworth 70-pounder guns, the armor plated ships were designed not only to break the blockade but to attack port cities in the North.

Heretofore, Union officials had to be somewhat circumspect in complaining to the British government about Confederate purchase operations in England. After all, Union agents often competed for the same arms and equipment offered for sale. However, the construction of the Laird Rams combined with the depredations of the raider CSS *Alabama*, which by then had captured or destroyed thirty-seven Northern ships, so terrified United States military and political leaders that they put tremendous political pressure on the British government to prevent the rams from ever sailing under Confederate colors.

Charles Adams' letter of September 5 to Lord Russell was blunt; England must impound the rams or face war with the United States:

In the present state of the harbor defenses of New York, Boston, Portland, and smaller Northern cities, such a vessel as the "Warrior" would have little difficulty in entering any of those ports, and inflicting a vital blow...The destruction of Boston alone would be worth a hundred victories in the field...Vessels of the Warrior class would promptly raise the blockade of our ports...It would superfluous in me to point out to your Lordship that this is war.

Bowing to the demands of the United States, the British government detained the ships and eventually seized them in 1864, paying the Confederate government fair value for them.

As the powerful chief financial officer for operations in England and Europe, Colin J. McRae quickly became aware of the weaknesses in the import/export system. He proposed that the government, not private concerns, should control all imports and exports, and that the government should also buy up all the cotton and tobacco at fair prices and then control the sale of those valuable commodities.

His recommendations were given full effect in February 1864 when the government passed laws that banned the shipment of cotton on private vessels without prior government approval, and controlled the importation of such non-essential civilian items as liquor, and jewelry. Henceforth, every privately-owned Southern ship was legally considered as being leased to the government for half its cargo space, both in and outbound.

In addition, the owners of private cargoes (mainly cotton) legally exported from the South had to bring back in military supplies worth half the value of what they had exported.

Colonel Gorgas appointed his brother-in-law, Major Thomas L. Bayne, to be in charge of ships for the Ordnance Department, and put James M. Seixas in control of operations at the all-important port of Wilmington, North Carolina. Those changes resulted in a vastly improved flow of government cargoes, and military blockade running reached its zenith in 1864–1865.

With the capture or blockade of some of the other ports, Wilmington became the main loading point for government cotton and the importation of supplies until its fall on January 16, 1865. In addition to a secure, guarded location on the Cape Fear River, the town had a large cotton press that was able to compress up to five hundred bales per day. So important was the operation there that Judah P. Benjamin estimated that the annualized 1863 exports from the city were $21 million, almost five times the total foreign commerce of the entire state of North Carolina just five years earlier.

At long last the Confederacy's "White Gold" was being properly utilized, and privately-owned ships became of more use to the military. But despite those changes, the government still relied heavily upon sharing cargo space in the civilian ships for transportation of much of the military supplies, and steep freight costs continued to add up. George Alfred Trenholm's not unreasonable explanation was that if one of his ships was captured the government merely lost only its portion of the cargo, but Fraser, Trenholm lost an entire ship, the value of its cargo and all future profits.

It was evident that the government needed a larger fleet of its own non-profit ships. In July 1864 Richmond officials ordered the purchase of fourteen steel steamships, each capable of running at thirteen knots and carrying one thousand bales of cotton. That ambitious plan, however, was never completed in time.

CHAPTER EIGHT

Blockade Running From the Islands

ALTHOUGH the *Bermuda* was the first ship to sail from England to the Confederacy with a military cargo, it was the October 1861 voyage of the John Fraser ship *Theodora* that became the prototype for blockade runners during the rest of the war.

Departing from Charleston on October 12, the ship's mission was simply to deliver James Mason and John Slidell, the Confederate commissioners to England and France, to Cuba, where they were to board a faster ship to Europe. While there, it was decided to return the ship to Charleston loaded with a diverse cargo of swords, pistols, coffee, and twenty thousand Cuban cigars. The goods were useful, of course, but the voyage clearly demonstrated that fast, shallow draft vessels were ideal for carrying cargoes between Southern ports and the islands.

Previously, British merchants who saw the tremendous profits to be earned in blockade running sent their large merchant ships directly to the South from ports in England, Europe or from Bermuda and Nassau. For protection against United States blockading ships, cargo vessels usually sailed with papers listing Nassau or some other neutral port as the supposed terminus of the voyage. For the sake of appearance, the ships often made short calls at those ports.

The United States Navy was not deceived, however, and began an aggressive policy of seizing all the foreign vessels they could that were carrying forbidden cargoes. Their actions were based upon the *Doctrine of Continuous Voyage*, a legalism accepted in United States prize courts, that said simply stopping at a neutral port in mid-voyage did not eliminate the illegality of the entire voyage. Henceforth, the British flag no longer guaranteed immunity for the shipping of Confederate supplies.

With England neutral and accessible to the Confederacy, it became evident that her Bermuda and Bahama islands were ideal bases for supply. It was far safer for English merchants to have their British-registered ships sail to British ports in those islands and unload their cargoes. After all, no laws were violated if they sailed cargoes to one of their own ports, even if the harbors were filled with the newly developed class of Confederate blockade running ships, carrying cotton to the islands and returning South with cargoes off-loaded from British ships.

The islands were conveniently located to Southern ports: Wilmington was only 570 miles from Nassau[1] and 674 miles from Bermuda. Even the more distant Southern ports could be reached in reasonable sailing times. As well, the people and governments of the islands were amenable to the arrangement. The white residents descended mainly from British stock or American Tories who settled there after the Revolutionary War, and they were hardly pro-Union in attitude. The local governments were British, and officials and residents alike eagerly anticipated the employment and revenues that would be generated as their islands became Confederate supply depots.

Confederate government relations with the islands were established in July 1861 when Charles J. Helm was appointed as "Special Agent of the Confederate States in Spanish, British, and Danish Islands of the West Indies."

Helm, based in Cuba at the time, where he had previously served three years as the United States consul, visited the British islands and quickly established a friendly rapport between the local governments and Richmond. In December, New Orleans businessman Louis C. Heyliger was appointed to the post of Confederate agent at Nassau, where he was later joined by Jean Baptiste Lafitte of Georgia, an employee of the omnipresent John Fraser & Co.

One of Heyliger's first tasks upon arrival was to handle the situation of the *Gladiator*. The British-registered and flagged ship was sitting in the harbor at Nassau with a cargo of some 20,240 Enfields, and barrels of gunpowder, cartridges, medical equipment, uniform cloth and blankets. United States Navy ships standing offshore had frightened the British captain from attempting to leave Nassau for the South, and Heyliger complained to the local British authorities.

Such activities by United States ships, he said, "would tend to cut off the trade" that the Confederacy intended to establish at Nassau. As a result, the island government granted Confederate ships the important right to "break bulk and transship." Thereafter, cargoes from British ships were off-loaded at Nassau and reloaded piecemeal onto Southern ships for the trip home.

When the *Gladiator's* captain attempted to return his ship to England, Heyliger, perhaps on the advice of Robert E. Lee's naval aide,

John Newland Maffitt, bought the ship on the spot and had the cargo divided into two parts.

Arrangements were then made by Adderly & Company, a Bahamian firm with close ties to John Fraser, to ship the important cargo on two of Trenholm's newer steamers, the *Cecile* and the *Kate.* The ships sailed to Mosquito Inlet, near present-day Fernandina Beach, Florida, where their cargoes were unloaded. The valuable supplies were transported inland just days before Union troops secured the area.

By 1862 Nassau had become the center of Confederate blockade running activities. From its excellent harbor, blockade runners could make the trip to or from Southern ports in just two or three days, and the once-sleepy town enjoyed a wave of prosperity. Activity on the docks centered on "...discharging [bales of cotton] into lighters, tier upon tier of it, piled high upon the wharves, and merchant vessels, chiefly under the British flag, loading with it."[2]

Close, amiable feelings between the Bahamian and Confederate governments were encouraged by the islands' pro-Southern governor, Charles John Bayley, C.B., whose efforts to encourage Southern trade included the elimination of duties charged on cotton arriving from the South and reduced tonnage charges on freight.

Of those developments a delighted Heyliger wrote: "You may readily imagine how intensely disgusted the Yankees are at this partiality, as they style it. My relations with the authorities here are of the most friendly character. I received marked attentions, which I value as going to show the increased cordiality of feeling toward the Confederate Government."[3]

Bermuda became a Confederate supply base during the summer of 1863 when Colonel Gorgas sent Major Norman S. Walker, his old friend and West Point classmate, to the island to be the local purchasing agent and to set up an Ordnance depot. Walker worked closely with S. G. Porter, an Ordnance Department official, and with local resident John Tory Bourne, who was appointed as the Confederate government's commercial agent at Bermuda.

As with Nassau, the quiet Bermuda town of St. George experienced boom times with the arrival of Confederate shipping. Money flowed like water, causing inflated prices for everything; one Southern officer trying to live there on his military pay complained that the cost of living was four times greater than in New York City.

Bermuda's governor, H. St. George Ord, was officially neutral but privately predisposed toward Southern activities, and most others on the island were more than helpful. British officers at the dock and on the ships at the Royal Navy base adjacent to Boaz Island "...were always friendly and more than civil to Confederates; being sometimes, indeed, too profuse in their hospitality."[4]

The five warehouses, each with its own small wharf, quickly filled with supplies coming from England and with the 600 to 800 bales of cotton brought in on each ship arriving from Confederate ports. Nassau, because of its two-day shorter sailing distance from the South, remained the most active transshipping port. In 1864 some 164 ships departed Nassau for Confederate ports, while only fifty-seven steamed from Bermuda.[5] However, with the loss of the Mississippi River in 1863, Bermuda became the prime resupply depot for the Confederate Trans-Mississippi army.

The new method of transshipping required a new class of ships. Lumbering merchantmen were easy prey for United States blockade ships, and so Secretary Mallory recommended the basic design for the innovative, purpose-built ships that were needed for the job. They were to have a large 200 to 300 ton cargo capacity, yet draw only ten feet of water when fully loaded. Main propulsion was from a steam-driven screw, and sails were fitted as auxiliary power. Crew size was about one hundred men, and if possible, the ships were to be armed with three large Whitworth guns but to otherwise avoid the appearance of men-of-war.

More than one hundred blockade runners were built in Britain between early 1862 and late 1864, and the design that evolved during the war resulted in a ship that was typically about 180 feet long with a twenty-two foot beam. It had steam-powered sidewheels which drew less water than a propeller and provided speed well in excess of much of the United States blockade fleet.[6] The ships rode very low in the water and many had telescoping funnels which could be lowered to further reduce their visibility to the enemy. Burning smokeless coal and often painted a dull color, blockade runners were the stealth ships of their day.

Blockade running ships usually sailed under the British flag with British crews; officers were often Royal Navy officers working under various noms de guerre to disguise themselves. Crews sailed for glory and money, for at its peak blockade runner pay was fabulous. For a round trip, a captain could easily receive £1,000 ($5,000) in gold, the vitally important chief engineer and pilot got £500 ($2,500), second and third officers got £150 ($750). Even ordinary seamen received £50 ($250).

The potential profits for almost any item brought into the South were so great that crew and officers alike filled every available space with the scarce necessities and luxuries that were cheap to buy in England but which commanded astronomical sums in the South.

One captain enjoyed particular success with a stack of corset stays he sold for a 1,100 percent profit, and toothbrushes that brought 700 percent. Outward bound, the officers crammed their cabins full of personal supplies of cheaply-acquired cotton, which they sold in England or the islands for equally great profits.

During the early and middle parts of the war the blockade was so loose that at times there could be as many as twenty blockade runners in Charleston harbor. Sailing schedules were so regular they were advertised in the newspapers. A resident of Mobile noted that one such blockade runner made voyages "almost as regular as a mail-packet in time of peace,"[7] while an English visitor at Wilmington in June 1863 said the twelve blockade runners he saw at the wharves "shows the absurdity of calling the blockade an efficient one."[8]

The crews ran no great risk if captured. British crewmen were simply detained just long enough to testify at the prize trials for their ships, and when released they usually returned to Bermuda or Nassau and joined another ship. Southern crewmen, however, were considered prisoners of war and were sent to military prisons.

As for the ships themselves, occasional losses were regarded simply as a cost of doing business. The trade was so lucrative that Seth Hawley, United States consul at Nassau, reported that as soon as one blockade runner was captured another came to replace it.

Although the Confederate government eventually established its own shipping, throughout the war, and particularly so in the first two years, Huse and the other agents had to constantly fight for high-priced cargo space aboard private vessels. The owners of the commercial ships did of course transport government supplies, but they preferred high-profit civilian cargoes.

Quinine, for example, took up very little space but sold in the South for $400 to $600 an ounce. English books, always prized in the South, were in high demand, as was almost everything necessary to normal life. Even ordinary items such as steel pen nibs and coffin screws had to come in through the blockade, and all those items competed for cargo space with Enfield rifles, cartridges, and uniforms.

Luxuries were also in great demand and provided maximum profits to the shipping companies. For example, when the steamer *Minho*, owned by the Navigation Company of Liverpool, ran aground off Sullivan's Island, South Carolina, in October 1862, her cargo was recovered and brought good prices at auction in Charleston. A partial list of the items included six hundred ninety-eight barrels and cases of champagne, wines, and other spirits; twelve hundred wine glasses; seventeen hundred tumblers; cigars; coffee and tea pots; cooking pans; medicines; shoes; and a considerable quantity of gilt military buttons.[9]

Although the agents and shipping company owners normally concerned themselves only about major cargoes, from time to time they had to devote both valuable cargo space and their personal time to accommodate pleading requests from friends and family members who needed items no longer available in the South.

In March 1862 Charles K. Prioleau, Fraser, Trenholm's partner in Liverpool, received a pleading letter and a list of things needed by a friend in Charleston. The items included: Brown Windsor soap, 1 dozen toothbrushes, some paper envelopes, a few pounds of green tea, gout medicine, and Mother Goose melodies.[10] The friend concluded his list by requesting the items be sent to him by "...any vessel in your employ coming this way—to run the blockade or otherwise." Undoubtedly, the items were sent.

John Fraser & Co. was the largest and most successful blockade running company, but there were many others in the South or in England, some of which were capitalized at over $1 million. The risks in the trade were great, but so were the potential profits. Hawley estimated that the average blockade runner would be lost or captured after four voyages, but even including the loss of the ship and its final cargo it would have returned a net profit of some $276,000.

Of course, many ships successfully ran the blockade numerous times without being captured. One of them, the *Hattie*, ran in and out of the blockade sixty times, usually in broad daylight.[11]

Despite a tightening blockade, Trenholm said by the end of 1864 only about ten percent of the cotton shipped out was captured, and in the last quarter of 1864 twenty-three out of twenty-six ships successfully ran through the heavy blockade at Wilmington. Stock in blockade running companies continued to soar in value, and even at that late date shares that originally cost $1,000 were in some cases trading for as much as $30,000.

There is wide variation in the estimates, but including ships of all kinds there may have been as many as 8,300 successful runs through the blockade during the war.[12] About 84 percent of the 2,054 recorded attempts to run the blockade into ports along the North and South Carolina coasts from April 1861 to February 1865 were successful.[13]

CHAPTER NINE
Best-Clad Army in the World

EVEN though the Northern blockade grew stronger, by 1864 a greater flow of supplies came into Southern ports than ever before. McRae in London noted that Confederate credit in England "...again begins to look up," and by February Governor Vance of North Carolina could boast that his state's troops were better clothed and armed than at any other time during the war.

Just a month earlier, he had either at Bermuda or bound for there eight to ten cargoes of stores for his troops, including forty thousand blankets and a similar amount of shoes, large amounts of uniform cloth and leather, and machinery to refurbish the state's cotton mills. The state-run operation was so successful and profitable that Vance even tried to set up a separate arrangement with Alexander Collie & Co. until Secretary of War Seddon put a stop to it.

In March, Major Bayne was promoted to lieutenant colonel and put in charge of the Bureau of Foreign Supplies, giving him tremendous control over imports and exports. Backed by the powerful new laws that restricted civilian imports and exports, Bayne was at long last able to implement procedures that resulted in a greater amount of military supplies coming in. Within a month he was importing large amounts of blankets, meat, shoes, and other supplies.

By July, Alexander Collie & Co. received a contract to supply £200,000 worth of clothing, quartermaster stores, and medical supplies. By fall, the availability of supplies and shipping was apparently so good that even small items could be given attention. Major J. B. Ferguson[1] was asked to obtain "a cheap and serviceable felt hat that would be very acceptable to the army,"[2] and then to "purchase liberally of material for officers' uniforms." As to the latter, Anderson was to look for cloth that was sturdy and available in quantity. As well, he was authorized to export some five thousand yards of superior-quality officers' cloth "for special purposes."[3]

Major Richard P. Waller, Confederate agent in Nassau, was ordered to cease buying in the islands because Ferguson found that goods of a better quality were priced cheaper in England. On September 29 Gorgas noted in his diary that despite some reverses in the field, from a resource standpoint "Really we are better off now than we were two years ago," and that the only real lack was "The scarcity of men to fill up our ranks."[4]

Meat was also imported in great quantity, with the first purchase of 2,989,944 pounds of bacon occurring in May 1863. Those imports would increase during the war, with some 8,632,000 pounds of meat delivered into the ports of Charleston and Wilmington alone for the thirteen months ending in December 1864.

By that time the Army of Northern Virginia and most of the other troops in the Southeast received the bulk of their meat, the so-called "Bermuda Bacon," via circuitous routes through the blockade. One guise was for foreign-flagged ships to purchase meat in Boston or New York, then sail to Canada for a short time before traveling on to Bermuda or the Bahamas. There, the meat was resold at Confederate warehouses for two to three times the original cost and blockade runners then took it into Southern ports. Another route was for the ships to sail directly from Northern ports to Liverpool, from where the meat was sent to the islands.

Quite literally, Billy Yank and Johnny Reb enjoyed the same beef that was originally processed in Chicago or Cincinnati.[5]

By December, the numbers of blockade runners entering Southern ports were increasing and averaged more than one arrival per day at Charleston and Wilmington. Gorgas reported that "they had no difficulty in importing arms through the blockaded sea-port," and that for the year 1864 46,254 rifles, pistols, and carbines were imported, compared to the 20,485 manufactured in Confederate arsenals.[6]

Confederate bureaucrats also needed supplies, so along with military goods blockade runners brought in large amounts of nineteenth-century office supplies. One delivery for the Navy Department included: letter paper, foolscap, notepaper, 25,000 official envelopes, 10,000 letter envelopes, record books, book presses, penknives, erasers, ink stands, and twenty gallons of the "best recording ink."

During the last half of 1864 through late January 1865, the 72,000 men of the Army of Northern Virginia received 104,900 jackets, 140,578 pairs of trousers, 167,862 pairs of shoes, 146,136 pairs of socks, 74,851 blankets, 4,861 overcoats, 27,011 hats, 170,000 pairs of drawers, and 178,790 cotton and flannel shirts.[7]

The 25,000-man Army of Tennessee received 45,000 jackets, 100,000 pairs of trousers, 100,000 pairs of shoes, 27,000 blankets, and 60,000 shirts.[8] Much of those finished goods, or the materials to make them, came through the blockade.

With such an outpouring of supplies, it is no wonder that on October 30 the sarcastic Richmond bureaucrat John B. Jones admitted to his diary that "immense amounts of quartermaster stores" were arriving at Wilmington, and that "perhaps our armies are the best-clad in the world."[9] With supplies flooding in, Jones, who previously had complained of outrageous prices for civilian shoes in Richmond, paid just $10.00 for a pair of imported British army shoes which he found to be "Most excellent in quality."

Foreign manufacturers continued to increase the supply of ready-made Confederate uniforms. In August, Bayne wrote to George Alfred Trenholm, who was by then serving as Secretary of the Treasury, saying that the firm of Rosenberg & Haiman would deliver 100,000 uniforms and like number of pairs of shoes to Liverpool. And on Christmas Eve a large quantity of uniforms made by the Irish firm of Peter Tait & Co. arrived in Wilmington.

Lacking the factory resources of the North, many of the Confederate army's uniforms had heretofore been made by a cottage industry of Southern women working in their homes with cloth provided by government contractors. The women were paid on a piece-rate basis, but production was sporadic and there was considerable variation in the workmanship and sizing of the finished uniforms.

Tait's appeal to the Confederate army was in his company's ability to produce quantities of uniforms. He had earlier pioneered the concept of large-scale manufacturing of high-quality, standard-sized uniforms, and his reputation was earned during the Crimean War when the two thousand employees of his factory in Limerick, Ireland, produced thousands of uniforms for the British army in a very short period.

Later, in one six-week period in early 1863 and on very short notice, Tait was able to manufacture and ship 21,000 complete uniforms for the Canadian army.[10]

Peter Tait himself had met with the Canadian adjutant general in London to obtain that contract, and most likely Confederate agents there knew or had heard about his company's abilities in that regard.

The Confederate uniform jackets Tait produced were essentially a shortened version of the standard British army jacket of the time. Supplied in a number of accurate sizes in the regulation cadet gray color of the Confederate army, many of the well-made jackets included appropriate branch-of-service facings and attached buttons.[11]

The uniforms were shipped to Wilmington aboard the *Evelyn*, one of three fast paddle wheel blockade runners owned by Tait. Much to the delight of the people of Limerick, the *Evelyn* ran unscathed through the heavy Union blockade both ways on her voyage, returning home loaded with cotton.

Even though these and the other government blockade running operations were at their peak, the war on land was rapidly coming to an end. For some time, Wilmington had become the most important of the remaining Southern ports. The city had a secure location on the Cape Fear River, some twenty miles upstream from where the river entered the Atlantic at two widely separated places, the New Inlet and the Old Inlet. The unique geography meant that Union blockade ships had to patrol fifty miles of shoreline, while land assaults were prevented by massive Fort Fisher, the "Gibraltar of the South." Located at New Inlet, it was linked to a system of thirteen smaller batteries and forts located along the river.

From the docks of the safeguarded city flowed the food and munitions desperately needed by Lee's army. Thus, the capture of the port became a priority for the North. On December 24, 1864, more than six hundred guns aboard fifty-six United States Navy ships commenced a furious bombardment of the fort, to be followed by the landing of a large combined force of sailors and soldiers to attack the fort. Despite their almost fifteen to one advantage in artillery and manpower, Northern forces were repulsed by the fort's undermanned garrison.

However, a larger Union returned on January 13, 1865. Fort Fisher was finally captured two days later, after some of the most vicious fighting of the war. Wilmington itself was soon in Union hands, its capture sealing the fate of the Confederacy. Confederate government import/export activity and purchasing operations everywhere came to an abrupt halt.

Offices in the islands closed, goods stored in warehouses there were returned to England, and government-owned blockade running ships sailed back to English ports. Financial disaster would soon strike a number of English mercantile houses. During the last six months of the war the Confederate government bought $45 million worth of supplies on credit overseas, and the collapse rendered Fraser, Trenholm unable to pay those immense debts.

It was all over.

CONCLUSION

IN the beginning, Southern hopes were high that England would take the Confederacy's side and intervene directly in the war. When that became an impossibility, England nevertheless remained a willing military warehouse for the South. Clearly, English and European sources of supply played major roles in sustaining Confederate military operations.[1]

Throughout the war, and increasingly so beginning in 1863, Confederate soldiers to a considerable degree were apt to be armed and uniformed with English-made goods that were run through the blockade in English ships with English crews. The incomplete records that survive make it impossible to determine the exact amounts of military imports to the Confederacy, but the quantities were obviously vast. Therefore, given the extent of these operations, one must wonder whether the now-mythical image of the "ragged rebels"—barefoot soldiers in homespun jackets—is wholly accurate.

Literally everything needed or used by Confederate soldiers, including food, was imported in such volumes that after the war one of Beauregard's staff officers said that the value of military imports was at least $200 million. That was a staggering sum considering that in those days Huse could buy Enfield rifle-muskets complete with bayonet and scabbard for just $15.50 each.

Modern authorities now estimate that some 500,000 to 600,000 small arms were imported, as was the majority of key Confederate supplies of uniforms and uniform cloth, edged weapons, leather, cartridge paper and lead. The importation figures combined with domestic production lends credence to comments of numerous Confederate officers that their men were generally well-equipped under normal circumstances.

Indeed, a few days after the battle at Chancellorsville in May 1863, a British observer noted that victorious Confederates had left: "...an enormous pile of excellent [captured] rifles rotting in the open air...the Confederates have already such a superabundant stock of rifles that apparently they can afford to let them spoil."[2]

In late 1864 the Army of Northern Virginia was apparently well enough supplied with shoes that General Lee returned fifty thousand pairs of them because of poor quality,[3] while the Confederate navy had on hand enough imported cloth to provide every man with a complete new uniform.[4]

Lieutenant Colonel W. W. Blackford served throughout the war as a staff officer and later wrote:

> In books written since the war it seems to be considered the thing to represent the Confederate soldier as in a chronic state of starvation and nakedness. During the last year of the war this was partially true, but previous to that time it was not any more than falls to the lot of all soldiers in an active campaign. Thriftless men would get barefooted and ragged and waste their rations to some extent anywhere...

If, as seems likely, Blackford's observation was correct, then the fighting efficiency of the Confederate army was due in no small part to the substantial flow of supplies that came through the blockade. Although unsung today, Gorgas, Huse, Trenholm, and the others who made that import system work, were of immense value to the South. Those men deserve the respect of history.

EPILOGUE

MAJOR Edward C. Anderson: Returned to Savannah to become the city's first post-war mayor, and went on to serve five more terms. At various times he was also a navigation consultant to the city, president of a steamship line, owner of an insurance agency, and held memberships in numerous boards of directors and educational, religious and historical societies in that city. He died on January 6, 1883, at age sixty-eight.

James Dunwoody Bulloch: Remained in England, where his family joined him after the war. He became active in the cotton brokerage business and also wrote the two-volume *The Secret Service of the Confederate States in Europe,* one of the best accounts of the attempts to organize the navy from European resources. His half-sister married Theodore Roosevelt, Sr., and was the mother of President Theodore Roosevelt. Bulloch never returned to the United States and died in England on January 7, 1901.

Alexander Collie: The partnership with the Crenshaw brothers dissolved in February 1864 due to disagreements between the partners and the loss of a number of their ships. Collie continued blockade running until the very end, even purchasing new ships, but the collapse of the Confederacy destroyed his company.

Cotton: Still a vital commodity, production and exports of cotton have increased greatly since the Civil War. In a typical year, about forty percent of the United States cotton crop is exported, bringing in not guns but some $2.5 billion in foreign revenues.

Captain William G. Crenshaw: Somewhat abrasive, Crenshaw seemingly irritated many of those with whom he came into contact. His own blockade running activities for the government continued after the breakup with Collie, and after the war he resumed a successful business career.

70

Firmin & Sons: The company remains in business to this day, supplying military forces around the world with a wide selection of buttons and other accouterments. They still have their original Confederate button moulds.

Erlanger Bondholders: When the war ended, English and European bondholders naively believed they had a right to the cotton that had been pledged as security for the bonds. However, Federal officials seized the cotton and declared that Confederate foreign contracts had no basis in law and were void. The bonds became worthless, but as of this writing dealers in collectibles are offering them for $2,000.00.

Fraser, Trenholm & Company: The partners in the several Trenholm companies were relentlessly hounded by United States government lawsuits filed in America and England, seeking to recover damages on the grounds that the company and its officers owed import duties on all the goods they imported during the war. The post-war Tribunal of Arbitration in Geneva said:

> ...if Fraser, Trenholm & Company had ceased to sell insurgent cotton and to convert it into money for the use of Huse, Heyliger, and Walker, the armies of the insurgents must have succumbed.

The combined pressure of creditors' lawsuits and the government's seizure of the assets of the companies and their officers ultimately forced the companies into bankruptcy. Corporate records, which could have provided a wealth of information about Confederate blockade running and finance, were burned after the war.

Major Josiah Gorgas: Rising to the rank of brigadier general in 1864, after the war he engaged in an unsuccessful venture as superintendent of the Brierfield Iron Works in Alabama. In 1869 he went on the staff of the University of the South in Tennessee, eventually becoming its vice chancellor. He became president of the University of Alabama in 1878, but ill health a year later forced him to resign that post. He continued on as the university's librarian, a position held until his death on May 15, 1883.

Captain Caleb Huse: Promoted to major during the war, he did not return to the United States until about 1868. Penniless, and with a large family, he had several unsuccessful business ventures until 1876, when he established an academy at Sing Sing, New York, to prepare candidates for admission to West Point. The school ran successfully for some twenty years, and Huse died in 1905.

S. Isaac, Campbell & Company: Although ultimately discredited by the Confederate government, the company was in great part responsible for the huge flow of supplies that sustained the Confederacy. While unethical, the company's behavior was hardly unusual for the contractors that sold to either side during the war. When others demanded cash in advance, S. Isaac, Campbell advanced their own money to the Confederacy, patiently waited for payment, and at the end were willing to accept at full face value the Confederate securities which led to their ruination. The company went bankrupt in the 1860s, leaving no records.

Henry Hotze: In 1868 he married the daughter of Felix Senac, Confederate paymaster in Europe. Hotze and his wife moved between Paris and London several times, while he apparently continued a career in journalism. After his death in Switzerland on April 20, 1887, his widow moved to Washington, D.C.

Laird Rams: More work was done on the ships after their seizure by the British government, and in 1865 they were put into the fleet as HMS *Scorpion* and HMS *Wivern*. Rapidly improving naval technology quickly made them obsolete, although both ships survived into the twentieth century.

London Armoury Company: Estimates indicate the company produced some 150,000 Enfield rifles for the Confederacy. In June 1863 Huse advised McRae that he had been offered the sale of the company, and in January 1864 it was recommended to Gorgas that an unspecified arms factory in England be purchased. That may have been the same plant, but in any event the London Armoury Company ceased to exist within a few months after the war.

Colin J. McRae: He emigrated to Honduras after the Civil War, and reestablished himself in various agricultural and other mercantile businesses. He died there in February 1877.

Stephen R. Mallory: United States troops arrested him at midnight on May 20, 1865, and Mallory spent the next ten months in jail. He later returned to Pensacola and practiced law until his death on November 9, 1873.

Peter Tait & Company: Shortly after the Civil War the company changed its name to the Auxiliary Forces Clothing and Equipment Co. Ltd. They continued to supply uniforms and clothing to armies around the world, including the United States army during World War I. However, the company's fortunes varied greatly during the twentieth century, and it finally went out of business in the 1970s. Peter Tait himself enjoyed great prestige and wealth during his lifetime, serving as mayor of Limerick and receiving a knighthood for his services to industry and to his city.

George Alfred Trenholm: Became Secretary of the Treasury in July 1864, too late for his talents to be used to straighten out the tangled morass of Confederate government finances. After Lee's surrender, Trenholm was imprisoned for four months when he refused to pay a bribe Union officials demanded for his freedom. Most of Trenholm's personal and corporate property was seized by a vengeful United States government on the specious grounds of paying for "import duties" owed on the millions of dollars worth of goods shipped by his companies during the war. Despite severe obstacles, Trenholm resumed his business career, served in the South Carolina state government, and helped greatly with the rebuilding of Charleston, where he became a leading and distinguished figure. He died December 12, 1876. There are those who see parallels between his background and that of the fictional Rhett Butler.

APPENDIX

Representative List of Imported Confederate Military Supplies:

Acid
Artillery Pieces
Artillery Carriages
Axes and Pickaxes
Bacon
Bayonets
Beef
Beer
Belts
Belt Buckles
Binoculars
Biscuits
Blankets
Books
Boots
Bottles
Bricks
Brooms
Bullets, Balls
Bullet Moulds
Buttons
Candles
Canned Meat
Canteens

Cap Pouches
Cartridges
Cartridge Boxes
Chains
Cloth for Uniforms
Coal
Coffee
Copper
Cutlasses
Cutlery
Drawers
Eating Utensils
Engineers' Eqpt.
Files
Fish
Glue
Gunners' Eqpt.
Gunpowder
Harnesses
Hats
Haversacks
Horseshoes
Ink
Ink Stamps

Iron Beams
Knapsacks
Leather
Lumber
Manuals
Map Paper
Matches
Medical Eqpt.
Medicines
Mill Board
Needles
Nails
Officers' Braid
Overcoats
Paper
Percussion Caps
Pig Iron and Lead
Pins
Planks
Plates
Pork
Printing Presses
Printing Type
Railroad Track

Rank Badges
Revolvers
Rifles, Muskets
Rifle Slings
Saddles
Salt
Saltpeter
Scabbards
Screws

Ships
Shirts
Shoes
Shovels
Soap
Socks
Stationery
Steel
Sugar

Swords, Sabers
Tea
Thread
Trousers
Twine
Umbrellas
Uniforms
Wheels, Hubs
Wool

ENDNOTES

CHAPTER ONE

1. New Orleans and St. Louis, both of which soon fell to Union forces.
2. William H. Russell, *My Diary North and South* (London: 1863), vol.1, 179.
3. E. A. Pollard and C. B. Richardson, *Southern History of the War* (New York: 1866), 97, 212–213.
4. Richard I. Lester, *Confederate Finance and Purchasing in Great Britain* (Charlottesville: University of Virginia Press, 1977), 4.
5. John D. Richardson, *The Messages and Papers of Jefferson Davis and the Confederacy Including Diplomatic Correspondence 1861–1865*, 2 vols. (repr., New York: Chelsea House-Robert Hector, 1966), vol.1, xix.
6. *The National Almanac And Annual Record For The Year 1864*. (Philadelphia: George W. Childs, 1864), 585.
7. William C. Davis, *A Government Of Our Own* (New York: The Free Press, 1994), 175–176.
8. Peggy Robbins, "Caleb Huse," *Civil War Times Illustrated* (August 1987): 31.
9. Although pledged for the bonds, much of the cotton remained in the possession of the planters. After the war, United States Treasury agents seized millions of dollars worth of the cotton from individuals on the grounds that it was an asset of the Confederate government.
10. C. Vann Woodward, ed. *Mary Chestnut's Civil War* (New Haven: Yale University Press, 1981), 376.

CHAPTER TWO

1. Otto Eisenschiml, *The Hidden Face of the Civil War* (New York: Bobbs-Merrell Co., 1961), 14.
2. Richardson, Ibid., 45.
3. Catherine Anne Devoreux Edmonston, *Journal of a Secesh Lady*, ed. Beth G. Crabtree and James W. Patton (Raleigh: North Carolina Division of Archives, 1979), 36.
4. Jefferson Davis, *Rise and Fall of the Confederate Government*, Part 2 (New York: D. Appleton Co., 1912), 10.

5. *Official Records of the United States and Confederate Navies in the War of Rebellion* (Washington, D.C., Government Printing Office, 1894–1927), ser. 2, 2: 83–87. Hereafter referred to as *O.R.N.*

6. J. William Jones, D.D., *Christ in the Camp* (B. F. Johnson & Co., 1887), 148–151.

CHAPTER THREE

1. Edward Boykin, *Ghost Ship of the Confederacy* (New York: Funk & Wagnalls Co., 1957), 94.

2. Given its other burdens at that moment, it is possible that the government was simply unable to react quickly enough to the East India Company's willingness to accept government bonds backed by 40,000 bales of cotton as payment for the ships. Even if the Treasury Department could have provided the rapid financing needed to acquire the cotton from the growers, there may not have been enough Confederate ships available to transport the cotton overseas.

3. Ethel Trenholm Seabrook Nepveux, *George Alfred Trenholm and the Company That Went to War 1861–1865* (Charleston, 1973), 25.

4. On March 25, 1863, Gorgas wrote that it was generally believed that John Fraser & Co. had already made $9 million in imports, and that the Crenshaw import/export firm of Richmond was making "hundreds of thousands monthly." Frank E. Vandiver, ed. *The Civil War Diary of General Josiah Gorgas* (University, Ala.: University of Alabama Press, 1947), 27.

5. Two months earlier, on the orders of President Davis, Raphael Semmes had gone to the North on a successful trip to buy weapons and powder from arms dealers there.

6. Fort Sumter surrendered on April 14, 1861.

CHAPTER FOUR

1. *The War of the Rebellion: A Compilation of the Official Records of the Union and Confederate Armies* (Washington, D.C.: Government Printing Office, 1880–1901), ser. 4, 2: 344. Hereafter referred to as *O.R.*

2. Confederate production of small arms in the Richmond and Fayetteville arsenals totaled about fifteen hundred weapons per month at the same time. *O.R.*, ser. 4, 2: 622.

3. Ibid.

4. The "America's Cup," the premier award in ocean racing, was named for that yacht.

5. Among other things, S. Isaac, Campbell owned a shoe factory.

6. William B. Edwards, *Civil War Guns* (Secaucus: Castle Books, 1978), 94.

CHAPTER FIVE

1. Howard Jones, *Union in Peril* (Chapel Hill: University of North Carolina Press, 1992), 61.

2. Henry Steele Commager, *The Blue and the Gray* (Indianapolis: Bobbs-Merrill Company, 1973), vol. 2, 516.

3. Frank L. Owsley, *King Cotton Diplomacy*, 2nd ed. (Chicago: University of Chicago Press, 1959), 156.

4. *O.R.N.*, ser. 2, 6: 176–177.

5. Fitzgerald Ross, *Cities and Camps of the Confederate States*, ed. Richard Barksdale Harwell (Urbana: University of Illinois Press, 1958), 200. Ross, a British subject and professional soldier, was a captain of Hussars in the Imperial Austrian Army. He was one of a group of European officers who accompanied Lee and the Army of Northern Virginia in 1863.

CHAPTER SIX

1. *O.R.*, ser. 4, 1: 564–565.
2. Nepveux, Ibid., 33–34; *O.R.*, ser.4, 1: 623, 633–634.
3. Wise, Ibid., 50–51.
4. *O.R.*, ser. 4, 2: 863–865, 971–972, 1003–1005.
5. *O.R.*, ser. 4, 1: 623, 633–634.
6. Lester, Ibid., 156.
7. *O.R.N.*, ser. 2, 2: 179.
8. *Alabama Claims: Case of the United States* (Washington, D.C.,: Government Printing Office, 1872), 98.
9. Caleb Huse, *The Supplies of the Confederate Army* (Boston: T. R. Marvin & Son, 1904), 21.
10. *O.R.*, ser. 2, 2: 890–891.
11. The ship was not named for governor Z. B. Vance of North Carolina. Likewise, she is often mistakenly referred to by the names *A. D. Vance* or *Ad-Vance*.
12. *Alabama Claims*, Ibid., 114.

CHAPTER SEVEN

1. Since the typical Civil War infantryman went into battle carrying about forty cartridges, this effort by Huse filled the cartridge boxes of some 100,000 Confederate soldiers.
2. Edwards, Ibid., 93.
3. A warrant issued by Huse on January 3, 1863, covered 2,068,000 pounds of cotton.
4. About $826,000 in Confederate currency.
5. Sterling and Francs.
6. The Laird shipyard built the *Alabama* in 1862, as well as a number of blockade runners during the war.

CHAPTER EIGHT

1. Fifty to sixty hours sailing time.
2. John Wilkenson. *The Narrative of a Blockade-Runner* (New York: Sheldon & Co., 1877), 86.
3. *Alabama Claims*, Ibid., 94.
4. Wilkenson, Ibid., 147.
5. Wise, Ibid., 132.
6. In a December 1864 letter to Secretary of the Navy Gideon Welles, Admiral D. D. Porter commanding the Atlantic Blockading Squadron complained that "The new class of blockade runners is very fast, and sometimes come in and play around our vessels; they are built entirely for speed." E. Lee Spence, *Treasures of the Confederate Coast: The Real Rhett Butler & Other Revelations* (Miami/Charleston, Narwhal Press, Inc., 1995), "Spence's List" #1864-12-US-X-2, 357.
7. Arthur W. Bergeron, Jr., *Confederate Mobile* (Jackson; University Press of Mississippi, 1991), 116.
8. Ross, Ibid., 95.
9. Spence, Ibid, "Spence's List."
   #1862-10-US-SC/GA-1, 197–198.
10. Letter from Jacob Williman to Charles K. Priouleau, dated Charleston, March 26, 1862. Copy in the possession of Ethel Trenholm Seabrook Nepveux.
11. Robert Carse, *Blockade* (New York: Rinehart & Co., 1968), 264.
12. Owsley, Ibid., 262.
13. Carse, Ibid., 181.

CHAPTER NINE

1. Since late 1862, the purchasing agent in England for the Confederate Quartermaster Department.
2. *O.R.*, ser. 4, 3: 674–675.
3. Ibid.
4. Frank E. Vandiver, ed. *The Civil War Diary of Josiah Gorgas* (University, Ala.: University of Alabama Press, 1947), 143.
5. A Confederate artillery officer in early April 1865 noted that "a small supply of luscious canned beef, imported from England" added much to the otherwise dreary army rations. Carlton McCarthy, *Detailed Minutiae of Soldier Life in the Army of Northern Virginia 1861–1865* (Richmond:1882; repr., Lincoln, NE: University of Nebraska Press, 1993), 117.
6. *O.R.*, ser. 4, 3: 986–987.
7. Philip Katcher, *The Civil War Source Book* (New York: Facts on File, 1992), 214.
8. Wise, Ibid., 211–212.
9. John B. Jones, *A Rebel Clerk's War Diary*, ed. Earl Schenk Miers (New York: Sagamore Press, 1958), 441.
10. "Mr. Peter Tait's Army Clothing Establishment," *Limerick Chronicle,* May 30, 1863.
11. Alan Thrower, "Peter Tait of Limerick," Confederate Historical Society *Journal* 16, No. 4 (Winter 1988), 95–96.

CONCLUSION

1. In early 1864 Robert G. H. Kean, head of the Confederate Bureau of War, noted in his diary the view of a negotiator in England that "...he had met no Englishman who did not wish us success and none who was willing for Great Britain to interfere [in the war]." Robert G. H. Kean, *Inside the Confederate Government* (Baton Rouge: Louisiana State University Press, 1993), p. 129.
2. Francis Lord, ed. *The Fremantle Diary* (Boston, 1954), p. 176.
3. Robert Boyce, "A Short Look Back," *Camp Chase Gazette*, October 1994, p. 40.
4. Joseph T. Durkin, S.J., *Confederate Navy Chief: Stephen R. Mallory* (Columbia: University of South Carolina Press, 1987), 327.

FURTHER RESOURCES

The following books provide more information about various aspects of Confederate government blockade running and foreign supply operations:

James D. Bulloch, *The Secret Service of the Confederate States in Europe* (G. P. Putnam's Sons, 1884, 2 vols.).

Howard Jones, *Union in Peril* (University of North Carolina Press, 1992. ISBN 0-8078-2048-2).

Richard I. Lester, *Confederate Finance and Purchasing in Great Britain* (University of Virginia Press, 1977. ISBN 0-8139-0513-3).

Ethel Trenholm Seabrook Nepveux, *George Alfred Trenholm and the Company That Went to War 1861–1865* (Charleston, 1973). A revised edition of this book is now available. For details, write to Mrs. Nepveux at 717 Parish Road, Charleston, S.C. 29407.

Stephen R. Wise, *Lifeline of the Confederacy: Blockade Running During the Civil War* (University of South Carolina Press, 1988. ISBN 0-87249-799-2).

Two museums have excellent interpretive exhibitions about blockade running activities:

The Cape Fear Museum, located at 814 Market Street in the center of the historic district of Wilmington, North Carolina, has extensive displays of artifacts run through the blockade, as well as a diorama that depicts Wilmington's role as a blockade running center.

Twenty miles south of Wilmington, Fort Fisher Historic Site contains the impressive remnants of the fort that guarded the Cape Fear River, as well as a museum housing more artifacts from the period.

BIBLIOGRAPHY

Adams, Ephraim Douglas. *Great Britain and the American Civil War*, 1925; reprint, Glouster Massachusetts: Peter Smith, 1957.

Alabama Claims: Case of the United States. Washington, D.C.; Government Printing Office, 1872.

Anderson, Major Edward C. *Confederate Foreign Agent: The European Diary of Major Edward C. Anderson.* ed. W. Stanley Hoole. University, Alabama: Confederate Publishing Company, 1976.

Belohlavek, John M., and Lewis N. Wynne. eds. *Divided We Fall.* Saint Leo, Florida: Saint Leo College Press, 1991.

Bennett, William. W., D.D. *The Great Revival in the Southern Armies.* Richmond, 1877.

Bergeron, Arthur W., Jr. *Confederate Mobile.* Jackson, Mississippi: University Press of Mississippi, 1991.

Bermuda Inbound Custom Books. 1864–1866. Hamilton, Bermuda: Bermuda Archives.

Bill, Alfred Hoyt. *The Beleaguered City.* New York: Alfred A. Knopf, 1946.

Blackford, Lieutenant Colonel W. W. *War Years With Jeb Stuart.* Baton Rouge: Louisiana State University Press, 1993.

"The Blockade Runner Evelyn." *Limerick Chronicle*, February 11, 1865.

Boyce, Robert. "A Short Look Back." *Camp Chase Gazette*, October 1994.

Boykin, Edward. *Ghost Ship of the Confederacy, The Story of the Alabama and Her Captain Raphael Semmes.* New York: Funk and Wagnalls Company, 1957.

Bulloch, James D. *The Secret Service of the Confederate States in Europe.* 2 vols. New York: G. P. Putnam's Sons, 1884.

Carse, Robert. *Blockade.* New York: Rinehart & Company, Inc., 1958.

Civil War Naval Chronology 1861–1865. Washington, D.C.: Naval History Division, Navy Department, 1971.

Cochran, Hamilton. *Blockade Runners of the Confederacy*. Indianapolis: Bobbs-Merrill Company, 1958.

Commanger, Henry Steele. Vol.1 of The *Blue and the Gray*. 2 vols. Indianapolis: Bobbs-Merrill Company, 1973.

Cullop, Charles P. *Confederate Propaganda in Europe 1861–1865*. Coral Gables: University of Miami Press, 1969.

Davis, Jefferson. *The Rise and Fall of the Confederate Government*, Part II, New York: D. Appleton Company, 1912.

Davis, William C. *A Government of Our Own*. New York: The Free Press, 1994.

Dupuy, R. Ernest and Trevor N. *The Compact History of the Civil War*. New York: Collier Books, 1960.

Durkin, Joseph T., S.J. *Confederate Navy Chief: Stephen R. Mallory*. Columbia: University of South Carolina Press, 1987.

Edmondston, Catherine Ann Devoreux. *Journal of a Secesh Lady*. Beth G. Crabtree and James W. Patton. ed. Raleigh: North Carolina Division of Archives, 1979.

Edwards, William B. *Civil War Guns*. Secaucus: Castle Books, 1978.

Eggleston, George Cary. *The History of the Confederate War*. 2 vols. New York: Sturgis & Walton Company, 1910.

Eisenschiml, Otto. *The Hidden Face of the Civil War*. New York: Bobbs-Merrill Company, Inc., 1961.

Foner, Philip S. *British Labor and the American Civil War*. London: Holmes & Meier Publishers, 1981.

Fremantle, Arthur J. L. *The Fremantle Diary*. Ed. Francis Lord. Boston, 1954.

Gaidis, Henry L. "Confederate Ordnance Dream: Josiah Gorgas, CSA, and The Bureau of Foreign Supplies." *North South Trader* 10, No. 1 (November–December 1982): 6–31.

Goff, Richard D. *Confederate Supply*. Durham: Duke University Press, 1968.

Gottschalk, Phil. *In Deadly Earnest*. Columbia, Missouri: Missouri River Press, Inc., 1991.

Gragg, Rod. *Confederate Goliath*. New York: HarperCollins Publishers, 1991.

Huse, Caleb. *The Supplies for the Confederate Army: How They Were Obtained in Europe and How Paid For*. Boston: T. R. Marvin & Son, 1904.

Jones, Howard. *Union in Peril*. Chapel Hill: University of North Carolina Press, 1992.

Jones, Rev. J. William, D.D. *Christ in the Camp, or Religion in the Confederate Army*. B. F. Johnson & Co., 1887.

Jones, John B. *A Rebel War Clerk's Diary*. Ed. Earl Schenk Miers. New York: Sagamore Press, 1958.

Katcher, Philip, *Civil War Source Book*. New York: Facts on File, 1992.

Kean, Robert Garlick Hill, *Inside the Confederate Government*. Ed. Edward Younger. Baton Rouge: Louisiana State University Press, 1993.

Lester, Richard I. *Confederate Finance and Purchasing in Great Britain*. Charlottesville: University of Virginia Press, 1977.

Long, E. B. *The Civil War Day by Day*. Garden City: Doubleday & Co., 1971.

Martin, Asa Earl. *History of the United States*. Vol. 1. Boston: Ginn and Company, 1934.

Massey, Mary Elizabeth. *Ersatz in the Confederacy*. Columbia, South Carolina: University of South Carolina Press, 1993.

McCarthy, Carlton. *Detailed Minutiae of Soldier Life in the Army of Northern Virginia 1861-1865*. Richmond: C. McCarthy, 1882.

The National Almanac and Annual Record For The Year 1864. Philadelphia: George W. Childs, 1864.

National Cotton Council. *Cotton From Field To Fabric*. Memphis: 1994.

Nepveux, Ethel Trenholm Seabrook. *George Alfred Trenholm and the Company That Went to War 1861-1865*. Charleston: 1973.

The War of the Rebellion: A Compilation of the Official Records of the Union and Confederate Armies (O.R.). 130 vols. Washington, D.C.: Government Printing Office, 1880-1901.

Official Records of the Union and Confederate Navies in the War of the Rebellion (O.R.N.). 31 vols. Washington, D.C.: Government Printing Office, 1894-1927.

Owsley, Frank L. *King Cotton Diplomacy*. 2nd ed. rev. by Harriet Chappell Owsley. Chicago: University of Chicago Press, 1959.

Pollard, E. A., and C. B. Richardson. *Southern History of the War*. New York: 1866.

Richardson, John D., ed. *The Messages and Papers of Jefferson Davis and the Confederacy Including Diplomatic Correspondence 1861-1865*. 2 vols. New York; reprint, New York, Chelsea House-Robert Hector, 1966.

Robbins, Peggy. "Caleb Huse." *Civil War Times Illustrated*. August 1987, 31-40.

Robinson, Major William M. "The Confederate Engineers." *The Military Engineer* 124 (July-August 1930): 297-305; 125 (September-October 1930):410-420; 126 (November-December 1930): 512-517.

Ross, Fitzgerald. *Cities and Camps of the Confederate States*. Ed. Richard Barksdale Harwell. Urbana: University of Illinois Press, 1958.

Russell, William H. *My Diary North and South*. 2 vols. London, 1863.

Spence, E. Lee. *Treasures of the Confederate Coast: The Real Rhett Butler & Other Revelations*. Miami/Charleston: Narwhal Press, Inc., 1995.

Spencer, Warren F. *The Confederate Navy in Europe.* University, Alabama: University of Alabama, 1983.

Stephenson, Wendell H. and E. M. Coulter, eds. *A History of the South.* Vol. 7. "The Confederate States of America 1861–1865." Baton Rouge: Louisiana State University Press, 1950.

The Story of LCF. Limerick, Ireland, np, nd.

Sullivan, David M. "Phantom Fleet: The Confederacy's Unclaimed European-Built Warships." *Warship International*, XXIV (1, 1987): 12–32.

Sword, Wiley. *Firepower From Abroad: The Confederate Enfield and the LeMat Revolver 1861–1863.* Lincoln, Rhode Island: Andrew Mowbray, Inc., 1986.

"Mr. Peter Tait's Army Clothing Establishment." *Limerick Chronicle,* May 30, 1863.

Thomas, Emory M. *The Confederate Nation 1861–1865.* New York: Harper & Row, 1979.

Thompson, Samuel Bernard. *Confederate Purchasing Operations Abroad.* Chapel Hill: University of North Carolina Press, 1935.

Thrower, Alan. "Peter Tait of Limerick." Confederate Historical Society *Journal*, Vol. 16, No. 4 (Winter, 1988).

Vandiver, Frank E. *Confederate Blockade Running Through Bermuda 1861–1865.* Austin: The University of Texas Press, 1947.

————. ed. *The Civil War Diary of General Josiah Gorgas.* University, Alabama: University of Alabama Press, 1947.

————. *Ploughshares Into Swords, Josiah Gorgas and Confederate Ordnance.* Austin: University of Texas, 1952.

Wilkenson, John. *The Narrative of a Blockade-Runner.* New York: Sheldon & Co., 1877; reprint, New York: Time-Life Books, Inc., 1984.

Wise, Stephen R. *Lifeline of the Confederacy: Blockade Running During the Civil War.* Columbia, South Carolina: University of South Carolina Press, 1988.

Woodward, C. Vann, ed. *Mary Chestnut's Civil War.* New Haven: Yale University Press, 1981.

MAIN TOPIC INDEX

Adams, Charles, 21-22, 56
Adams, Robert, 15
Adderly & Co., 11, 60
Advance (ship), 51, 78
Alabama, 4
Alabama (ship), 8-9, 55
Alabama Claims, 22
America (yacht), 16, 77
Anderson, Maj. Edward C., 16-18, 46-48, 65, 70
Army of Northern Virginia, 65, 69
Army of Tennessee, 66

Bahama Islands, 59, 65
Baring Bros., 12
Bayne, Maj. Thos. L., 56, 64, 66
Bayley, John C., 60
Beauregard, Gen., P. G. T., 13, 68
Belgian Rifles, 46
Benjamin, Judah P., 56
Bermuda, 11, 58-61, 64-65
Bermuda (ship), 21, 46, 58
"Bermuda Bacon," 65
Blackford, Lt. Col. W. W., 69
Blakely Cannon, 48
Blockade, 6, 7, 9, 61-63, 65, 67
Blockade Runners, 61, 63, 65, 67, 78
Boaz Island, 60
Bourne, John Tory, 60
British East India Co., 12, 77
British & Foreign Bible Society, 9
Bulloch, Cdr. James D., 8-9, 14, 17-18, 21-22, 46, 48, 54-55, 70
Bur. of Foreign Supplies, 64

Campbell, S. Isaac & Co., 17-18, 49-51, 54-55, 71, 77
Cecile (ship), 60
Charleston, 2, 7, 11, 58, 62, 65
Chestnut, Mary, 5
Collie, Alexander, 49, 64, 70

Collie-Crenshaw, 49-50
Columbia (ship), 53
Commerce Raiders, 21
Confederate Bible Society, 9
Cotton, 2-3, 53-54, 61, 63
"Cotton Famine," 3
"Cotton is King," 2-3
Crenshaw, Capt. Wm. G., 49-52, 70, 77

Davis, Jefferson, 4, 7, 16, 18
"Doctrine of Continuous Voyage," 58

Economist (London), 55
Enfield Rifle, 8, 15-16, 46-48, 59, 62, 68
Engineer Bureau, Confed., 13, 51
England, 2-3, 4-5, 8, 12-13, 19-21, 48, 53, 55-56, 58-59, 65, 68
Erlanger & Co., 54
Erlanger Loan, 52, 54-55, 71
Eugenie (ship), 53
Evelyn (ship), 67

Fayetteville Arsenal, 53, 77
Ferguson, Maj. J. B., 50-51, 64
Fernandina, Fla., 60
Fingal (ship), 48
Firmin & Sons, 71
Florida (ship), 9
Foreign Enlistment Act, 21
Fort Fisher, 67
France, 2, 4, 7-8
Fraser, John & Co., 11-12, 58-59, 63, 77
Fraser, Trenholm & Co., 9-12, 15, 21-22, 46, 48, 54, 63, 67, 71

Gayle, Amelia, 13
Genoese Muskets, 18
Gladiator (ship), 59
Gladstone, William, 55
Gloire (ship), 8

85

Gorgas, Maj. Josiah, 4, 13, 48, 51, 56, 60, 65, 69, 71, 77
Government Finances, 4-5, 12, 53-54, 56
Grant, Gen. U. S., 47

Hamilton, Archibald, 16, 47
Hampton, Wade, 46
Hattie (ship), 63
Hawley, Seth, 62-63
Helm, Charles J., 59
Heyliger, Louis C., 59-60
Hotze, Henry, 20, 72
Huse, Capt. Caleb, 13-18, 46, 52-54, 68, 69, 71

Imperial Austrian Arsenal, 53
Index, 20
Ironclad Ships, Conf., 8

Jones, John B., 66

Kate (ship), 60
Kean, Robert G. H., 79
Kerr Revolver, 16, 18
"King Cotton Diplomacy," 54

Lafitte, Jean Baptiste, 59
Laird Rams, 55, 71, 78
Lee, Gen. Robt. E., 13, 69
Lee, R. E. (ship), 53
Lincoln, Abraham, 6
Liverpool, 11, 14-15, 63, 66
London Armoury Co., 15, 72
Lorenz Rifles, 53
Loans, Government, 4-5

Maffitt, John Newland, 60
Mallory, Steven, 7-8, 48, 61, 72
Mann, A. Dudley, 7
Mason, James, 58
McCarthy, Carlton, 79
McRae, Gen. Colin J., 51-52, 55-56, 64, 72
Meat Imports, 65
Memminger, C. G., 4
Merrimac (ship), 53
Minho (ship), 62
Minna (ship), 48
Missouri Brigade, 47
Mobile, Ala., 2, 7, 62
Montgomery, Ala., 4, 13
Myers, Abraham C., 4, 6

Nassau, 11, 58-61, 65
New Orleans, 4, 7, 8, 76
North, Lt. James H., 8

Ord, H. St. George, 60
Ordnance Bureau, 4, 13, 17, 46, 56, 60

Pay, Ships' Crews, 61
Pinckney, Harriet, 13
Porter, S. G., 60
Prioleau, Chas. K., 63
Privateers, 7
Produce Loan, 4

Queen's Proclamation, 21, 46
Quinine, 62

Richmond Arsenal, 77
Robinson, Capt. James F., 51
Ross, Capt. Fitzgerald, 22, 77
Royal Navy Officers, 61
Russell, Lord John, 10, 21, 56

Sea-King (ship), 22
Seddon, James A., 16-17, 50, 64
Seixas, James M., 56
Senac, Felix, 72
Semmes, Capt. R. D., 8, 77
Shenandoah (ship), 9, 22
Sinclair, Hamilton & Co., 16
Slidell, John, 58
So. Independence Assn., 20
St. George, Bermuda, 60
St. Louis, Mo., 76
Sumter (ship), 8-9

Tait, Peter, 66, 72
Tait, Peter & Co., 66-67, 72
Tallahassee (ship), 9
Theodora (ship), 58
Times, London, 2
Tower Viewer, 18
Trenholm Bros., 11, 14
Trenholm, George A., 12-13, 57, 63, 66, 69, 72-73

Uniforms, 4, 17, 48-49, 52-53, 59, 62, 64-66, 68-69
United States Navy, 6-7, 58-59, 67

Vance, Gov. Zebulon, 64
Vicksburg, 47

Walker, Leroy Pope, 4
Walker, Maj. Norman S., 60
Waller, Maj. Richard P, 65
War Dept., Confederate, 47, 49-50
Warrants, Cotton, 49, 51, 54, 78
Warrior (ship), 56
Westbury, Lord, 19
Whitworth Cannon, 55
Wigfall, Louis T., 1-2
Wilmington, N.C., 7, 56, 59, 63, 65-67

Yancey, William L., 7